Responsibility and Self-Management

A Client Workbook of Skills To Learn

by Jack Apsche, Ed.D., ABPP
and Jerry L. Jennings, Ph.D.

Client's Workbook for Responsibility and Self-Management Skills

2nd Printing 2011

Published by
NEARI Press
70 North Summer Street
Holyoke, Massachusetts
01040 USA
413.540.0712

Distributed by
NEARI Distribution
888.632.7412

ISBN# 978-1-929657-29-2

Table of Contents

Acknowledgements

I would like to thank Joe Dunham for his great efforts in completing most of the client interviews for this workbook.

Editor and friend, I would like to thank Robert Longo. His support on this project was imperative in the completion of the Workbook and Clinician's Manual.

I especially want to thank my daughter Melissa Apsche. Her dedication and work in the completion and preparation of the Workbook and Clinician's Manual made these works possible.

Thank you to all of the clients I have worked with. You have taught me well.

Jack Apsche

INTRODUCTION TO CLIENT'S WORKBOOK

You are beginning a treatment program for youth who have harmed others or committed offenses. You will be learning a great deal about yourself and the behaviors that have gotten you into trouble. You will learn that you have certain negative beliefs and thoughts because of your past experiences in life. You will learn how thoughts and beliefs cause emotions and behaviors, including abusive behavior. That is why you must first change your beliefs and attitudes if you are going to make real and lasting changes that will reduce your risk of harming others in the future.

Deep-set negative beliefs about yourself can trigger many different negative thoughts, feelings, and behaviors that will lead you to act-out or harm others. The problem is that abusive persons are usually not aware of these deep-set beliefs. You probably do not know how negative thinking and negative beliefs are causing you to behave badly and hurt other people. With the help of your primary therapist and other counselors and staff, this workbook will show you how to overcome negative thoughts and beliefs that lead to abusing and lower your risk to act-out. You will learn how to deal with negative feelings, such as hurt, loneliness, shame, guilt, and inferiority. This workbook will be used in combination with group therapy and individual therapy to help you learn skills to control your anger, sadness and aggression in more healthy ways – and feel better about yourself.

You have a lot to learn. And it takes time to learn. People learn at different speeds, and some people find it easier to learn some things and harder to learn other things. The counselors and program staff are committed to helping you learn at your own pace. Even if you have been in treatment before, there is always more to learn to better yourself.

The first step is honesty. You have to be honest with yourself. You must recognize that you need to change and begin to take responsibility for your actions. You are in treatment because you have been abusive, acted-out and/or hurt other people – and you remain at high risk of doing it again if you don't change yourself. Plain and simple. It is time to stop making excuses for why you did it; time to stop pretending that the acting-out wasn't as bad as it really was. The more you can be honest with yourself and others, the more progress you can make.

Be patient. This workbook contains lots of good information. Take the extra time to learn the information well and practice it. Participate in treatment activities and do your best to finish the exercises and homework in this workbook – and it may help you to become a responsible person with self-pride, who cares for others and finds pleasure in life. This will be your own personal copy. You own it. You can write in it and keep it for review and reminders.

Good luck on your journey toward recovery and healthy, positive living.

Responsibility and Self-Management Skills

Intensive Treatment Phase

Level One
Gaining Knowledge

Treatment begins with "gaining" basic information and knowledge that will help in your recovery.

Level one will help you to understand the basic idea and rules of what is called "cognitive–behavioral" treatment. It means "thinking–behaving" treatment. This thinking–behaving model is the common "language" that everyone will be using in this treatment program. The counselors, staff and residents will use thinking–behaving language whenever we talk about issues and behavior. Thinking–behaving words will be used often and you will soon become familiar with the words and the way that thinking-behaving treatment works.

CHAPTER 1
NEGATIVE THINKING AND LEARNING TO WATCH YOURSELF

What Is Negative Thinking?

Acting-out, like all behavior, begins in your head. Thoughts are the beginning of your behavior. Your negative thinking causes your negative behaviors. This is true for all kinds of behavior. Negative thinking can overpower your sense of right and wrong and cause you to make up all kinds of reasons and excuses for acting badly and hurting other people.

This workbook will teach you how to "watch yourself" more closely. When you can learn to watch your own thoughts, feelings and behavior, you will then be in the position to change and control your behavior.

For example, let's say you come to your friend's home after school at the end of the day and see that one of your friends left his iPod™ lying on a table. You don't know for sure who owns the iPod™, but you think, "I want that iPod™. Hey, if he left his iPod™ out in the open, then he deserves to lose it." You think that you could sell it to another student or give it to your girl before anyone catches on.

What did you think when you pictured this situation? Yes, the guy would lose his iPod™. He'd be angry or upset. But you may tell yourself, "It's his tough luck. He shouldn't have left it out." The decision to steal the iPod™ is based on negative thinking. If you were thinking clearly, you would know that it is not right to steal someone else's property. But your negative thinking tells yourself that it's okay to steal the iPod™ – it's his fault for leaving it unprotected, not your fault for stealing it. Negative thinking tries to give you a good excuse for bad behavior.

Bad behavior is not the only thing caused by negative thinking. Rotten moods are also caused by negative thinking. Depression is one of those moods. You may have many negative thoughts when you are in a bad mood. You might think, "I'm no good. Nobody likes me. I can't do anything right. Nobody really cares about me." Your negative thinking starts to convince yourself that these thoughts are true facts about yourself – not just wrong opinions. When you think negatively, it actually makes you feel sad and depressed.

Can you remember a time when other kids or people picked on you or laughed at you? If no one took your side and defended you, you probably had a negative thought: that some of the mean things they said were really true about you. If they called you stupid, you might begin to believe you are stupid. If you were teased or insulted over and over, you may have felt sad or angry or wanted to hide from people. You may even have come to believe that you are a bad person who deserves to be treated badly. Negative thinking can be very harmful to your self-image and self-pride.

The exercises in this workbook will help you to begin to recognize when you are having negative thoughts – and that is the first step to stopping negative thinking. At this point, most of your negative thinking seems like it is automatic. It is like a bad habit. It happens very quickly and without your awareness. So you do not realize that you are thinking negatively.

Beginning now, you should try to write down your negative thoughts when you are aware that they happen. Usually we think "out loud" in our heads. We talk to ourselves. This is thinking. Your counselor and the treatment team will help you to learn to catch yourself having negative thoughts. So if you fail at something and say to yourself, "I don't understand because I'm stupid," you will stop for a second and realize that you just had a negative thought. When you think "I'm stupid," it causes you to feel bad about yourself and you may react with anger or wish to make someone else feel bad. By watching your inside thoughts, you will also begin to see how negative thinking is causing you to have negative feelings and rotten moods and to act negatively.

This is not easy. It takes time and practice. Here are some examples of negative thoughts. You may even have thought these same thoughts yourself.

- This treatment won't help...
- This place sucks...
- I'll never get out of this place…
- I'm too stupid to understand this...
- I'll never get through this workbook...
- I'll have a bad day...

Use this space to write down some of the negative thoughts you may have had today:

____

____

____

____

____

____

Negative Thinking and Negative Talk

You have learned that negative thoughts are negative statements that we say to ourselves inside our own heads. But negative thoughts can also take the form of negative statements that we say to other people. This is "negative talk." Negative talk includes cursing, dirty words, insults, threats, and inappropriate sexual comments. Negative talk goes hand-in-hand with negative thoughts, negative moods and negative behavior.

Now, in addition to writing down the negative words that you say to yourself (your negative thoughts), start to pay attention to the negative words that you say out loud too. Try to record your negative talk (said silently to yourself) and negative talk (said out loud to others) at the time that they occur. Later, you can examine your negative thoughts and statements and see how they are causing your negative feelings and negative behavior.

Example: You are feeling angry because some classmate made fun of you in math class for getting a problem wrong. You really were "pissed off" and told him to go f*** themselves and really went off on them! You said to yourself, "I can't get these problems right" and felt humiliated so you cursed out the student and teacher. A new way of thinking might be; "I got this problem wrong but, I can learn the assignment if I stay calm." You also could try again and with help most likely get the problem correct. "I can learn this with help!"

I'll never learn this!	This sucks!	I can do this if I want to!

Client completes these columns by himself:		This section may be completed with a therapist.
NEGATIVE THINKING (said silently to myself)	NEGATIVE TALK (said out loud to others)	NEW WAYS OF THINKING

How Thoughts, Feelings and Behavior Go Together

The Thinking, Feeling, and Behavior (TFB) Self-Report Sheet will be an important tool for learning to control your negative thinking. It will help you see how thoughts, feelings, and behaviors work together. Then you can start to change the negatives in your life into positives.

"Automatic Thoughts" are negative thoughts that occur very quickly in response to a situation. A particular event/thought/situation/emotion can trigger a thought so quickly that it seems like its automatic. There are many ways you can be triggered. It might be a memory, a smell, a taste, or just a perception. So, for example, when you see a female in a red dress, you may immediately think that "I want sex with her – so she must want sex with me."

Following the trigger, the first automatic thought can set off a series of negative thoughts, feelings and behavior that might look like this:

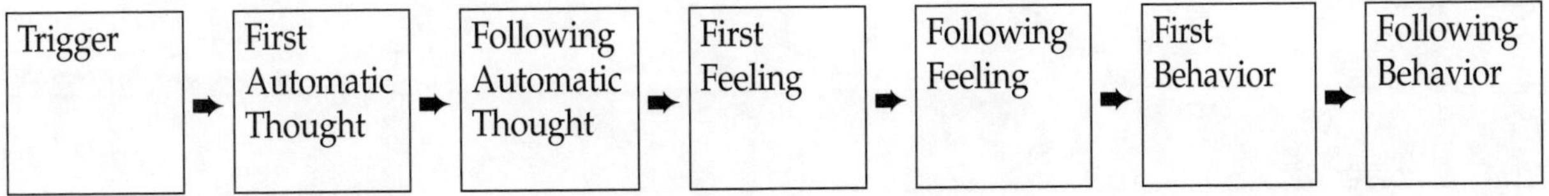

Let's look at each part of typical sequence:

Trigger ↓	A trigger is an event, situation, thought, feeling or mood that can "trigger" an automatic thought.
First Automatic Thought ↓	This is the first thought that pops into your head after the trigger event.
Following Automatic Thought ↓	This is a second thought that quickly follows the first thought.
First Feeling ↓	The first feeling, often negative, painful or disturbing, that goes along with the automatic thought(s).
Following Feeling ↓	A second feeling may follow the first feeling.
First Behavior ↓	The behavior that may follow the thought(s) and feeling(s). An example is: the first feeling is sadness; the first behavior is withdrawing from people to be alone in your room.
Following Behavior	A second behavior that may follow a first behavior. An example is: the first feeling is sadness; the first behavior is withdrawing, while the following behavior is breaking property in your room.

Instructions and Practice for Using the Thinking, Feeling, Behavior Self-Report Worksheet

TRIGGERS – Write down any triggers/situations/thoughts/feelings that you are aware of that affect your feelings and behavior. A trigger could be something you see (like a porno magazine or a person) or hear (like laughter or music) or smell (like smoke or food) or feel (such as being bored, sad, or down on yourself), or a situation (like taking a test or going to a party).

____

____

____

____

____

FIRST AUTOMATIC THOUGHT – Now write down the automatic thought that immediately comes to mind when you imagine one of your triggers. Write down the triggers in the left column and the first thought in the right column.

Trigger	First Automatic Thought
Gunshot	"I'll be killed."

FOLLOWING AUTOMATIC THOUGHT – Write down the second or "following" automatic thought that occurs after the trigger event. Write down the "trigger" in the left column, the "first thought" in the center column, and then the "following thought."

Trigger	First Automatic Thought	Following Automatic Thought
Gunshot	"I'll be killed."	"Someone is trying to kill me."

FIRST FEELING – Write down the first feeling (which is often negative, painful, or disturbing) that goes along with the automatic thought(s). Write down the "trigger" in the left column, then "first thought," then "following thought," then the "first feeling."

Trigger	First Automatic Thought	Following Automatic Thought	First Feeling
Gunshot	"I'll be killed."	"Someone is trying to kill me."	Fear

FOLLOWING FEELING – Write down the second or following feeling (which is often negative, painful, or disturbing) that follows the first feeling. Write down each component in the columns.

Trigger	First Automatic Thought	Following Automatic Thought	First Feeling	Following Feeling
Gunshot	"I'll be killed."	"Someone is trying to kill me."	Fear	Terror and panic

FIRST BEHAVIOR – Write down the first behavior that follows the thoughts and feelings. Write down each component in the columns.

Trigger	First Automatic Thought	Following Automatic Thought	First Feeling	Following Feeling	First Behavior
Gunshot	"I'll be killed."	"Someone is trying to kill me."	Fear	Terror and panic	Dive for cover.

FOLLOWING BEHAVIOR – Write down the second or following behavior that follows the first behavior. Write down each component in the columns.

Trigger	First Automatic Thought	Following Automatic Thought	First Feeling	Following Feeling	First Behavior	Following Behavior
Gunshot	"I'll be killed."	"Someone is trying to kill me."	Fear	Terror and panic	Dive for cover.	Remain in hiding place for very long time.

Several blank copies of the TFB Self-Report Sheet are included for practice. Additional photocopies can be provided as needed.

Thought, Feeling, and Behavior Self-Report Worksheet

This worksheet can be completed with your primary therapist, or in a group session, or as homework.

Trigger	First Thought	Following Thought	First Feeling	Following Feeling	First Behavior	Following Behavior

Thought, Feeling, and Behavior Self-Report Worksheet

This worksheet can be completed with your primary therapist, or in a group session, or as homework.

Trigger	First Thought	Following Thought	First Feeling	Following Feeling	First Behavior	Following Behavior

CHAPTER 2
COGNITIVE DISTORTIONS

Cognitive Distortions Defined

What is a "cognitive distortion"? The word "cognitive" simply means "thinking." And a "distortion" is an error or exaggeration. If something is distorted, it is not right. So the term "cognitive distortion" simply means an error in thinking. Cognitive distortions are thinking errors.

When you have errors in your thinking, you do not see life clearly and you make mistakes that have a negative effect on yourself and others. Everyone has some cognitive distortions, but abusive persons have lots of cognitive distortions.

These errors in thinking can have bad effects on your self-esteem, your relationships, your moods, and other areas of your life.

Imagine you are watching TV and the picture is out of focus. It is hard to understand what is happening when you cannot see the picture clearly. The picture is distorted. It's not the true picture. The same thing happens with thinking. If your thinking is distorted, you will have a messed up understanding of what is really happening and you will make mistakes that can hurt yourself and others. When you are angry, your thinking becomes distorted.

For example, a person is drinking heavily and says to himself, "I can have one more drink before I go home. It won't make much difference." This is a cognitive distortion – and it will lead to a bad mistake. The correct thinking should be: "I shouldn't drink and drive and having one more drink does make a difference." This is clear thinking – and will avoid a mistake.

Now let's take a look at some common types of cognitive distortions. Recognizing these cognitive distortions can help you better understand your problems and behavior. As you go through treatment, you will come across many of these cognitive distortions again and again. Remember that practice makes perfect. You will get better and better at recognizing cognitive distortions. This is a big step toward clear thinking and feeling positive.

Types of Cognitive Distortions

All or nothing: This cognitive distortion is looking at things in total black and white with no gray areas. Something is either the best thing that ever happened or the worse thing that ever happened. Something is either totally good or totally bad.

Examples: "Everybody lies. You can't trust anybody."
"If I fail at this, I quit."

Exaggerating: This cognitive distortion occurs when any negative event is seen as a horrible disaster or catastrophe. The person looks at a situation and exaggerates how bad it is or how bad it will be. The person will make the problem even bigger than it is. For example, the person will see one mistake or error that happened one time as proof that he will always screw up and fail.

Examples: "I got arrested. My whole life is over. I might as well be a criminal."
"If I screwed it up the first time, so there's no point in trying again."
"The therapist corrected me. I'm screwed in this program forever."

Seeing only the negative: This is the tendency to focus only on the negative and miss the positive. For example, a person who is court-ordered for treatment may only see that he is being punished, but it is also an opportunity to learn to be a better person.

Examples: "I flunked the test. I didn't learn anything from this class."
"I'm stuck in this rotten place. I can't do nothing but sit and wait."

Trashing the positive: This is the tendency to give oneself no credit for one's achievements or one's positive qualities as a person.

Examples: "So what if I got A's in school, it doesn't mean anything anymore."
"It doesn't matter if they like me now, it's only because they don't know me very well."

Mind reading: This is believing that one can guess what another person is thinking, or believing that you can predict what another person will do.

Examples: "I could tell by the way she looked at me that she didn't like me."
"If I ask her out, she will say no, so why should I bother to ask."

How I feel is how it is: This is a cognitive distortion in which the person thinks that the way they feel inside is the way others must also feel or that their mood is the actual truth of the situation.

Examples: "I feel like a thug, so I must be one."
"I feel hopeless so this must be a total disaster."
"I really want sex with her. She must really want sex with me."

Blaming yourself: This is a cognitive distortion in which the person blames himself for everything that goes wrong. Instead of seeing a mistake as a simple mistake, the person blames his whole personality. Instead of saying, "I made a mistake," he blames himself for being a "total idiot." The person puts a negative label on himself and then believes it is true. He labels himself as "stupid," or "ugly" or "perverted."

Examples: "Why did I say that? I'm such a jerk."
"Of course she said no. I'm ugly and stupid."

Blaming others: In this cognitive distortion, the person blames other people and events for his own mistakes and problems. It is usually used to avoid taking responsibility.

Examples: "I wouldn't be here if he didn't disrespect me."
"That therapist is too stupid to understand me."
"She didn't say no. I would've stopped if she did."

Making excuses: This is a cognitive distortion in which someone makes up a story or changes the facts or makes an excuse for having done something harmful. Sometimes the person will pretend that he didn't know or didn't understand that he was breaking the law or causing harm.

Examples: "I wouldn't have stolen the TV if he had locked his door."
"Someone abused me, so I did it to somebody else."
"It's not my fault that I forgot."
"I was drunk. I don't remember what I did."

Minimizing: This is making excuses by pretending that the offense or damage was less harmful than it really was.

Examples: "I only did it once. Come on, it's no big deal."
"I only slapped her. I didn't hit her with a closed fist."

Poor me: This is when a person "plays the victim." Instead of taking responsibility for abusing others, they blame their actions on the abuse that they have suffered or their difficult life. They see themselves as the victim rather than the victimizer. They may even try to get others to feel sorry for them so they will not be punished.

Examples: "Everyone always picks on me."
"Everyone always made fun of me."
"I was molested as a child. I thought that's how you show love."

There are many kinds of cognitive distortions. This list is only a few of the most common ones. Recognizing cognitive distortions is the first step. In the next exercise, we will practice the next step: learning ways to correct cognitive distortions.

Changing Cognitive Distortions With New Ways of Thinking

INSTRUCTIONS: In this exercise, we will take examples from each of the types of cognitive distortions and begin to think about changing or correcting them. Beside each of the following cognitive distortions, write down a new way of thinking that is positive.

Cognitive Distortions	New Ways of Thinking
All or nothing "Everybody lies. You can't trust anybody."	
Exaggerating "I got arrested. My life is over. I might as well be a criminal."	
Seeing only the negative "I flunked the test. So I didn't learn a thing from class."	
Trashing the positive "So what if I got A's in school, it doesn't mean anything now."	
Mind Reading "I could tell by the way she looked at me that she didn't like me."	
How I feel is how it is "I feel like a thug, so I must be one."	
Blaming yourself "Of course she said no. I'm ugly and stupid."	
Blaming others "I wouldn't be here if he didn't disrespect me."	
Making excuses "I wouldn't have stolen the TV if he had locked his door."	
Minimizing "I only did it once. Come on, it's no big deal."	
Poor Me "Everyone always picks on me."	

Chapter 3
Changing Negative Thinking

The Role of Cognitive Distortions in Abusing

Cognitive distortions are ideas and beliefs that are incorrect and lead to bad decisions, negative feelings and abusive behavior. Abusers have many cognitive distortions, which plays a big part in why they abuse others and usually feel bad about themselves. The good news is that clear, positive thinking leads to good decisions and positive actions.

Cognitive distortions are thoughts that "distort" the truth. Cognitive distortions often come from false or incorrect information. For example, abusers may use the following cognitive distortions to make an excuse for harming others. "If a woman says no, she really means yes." "A woman who hitchhikes is asking to be raped." "Peeping in windows doesn't really hurt anyone."

Cognitive distortions like these are at the core of acting-out. They are thoughts and beliefs that abusers use to escape responsibility for the harm they have caused to others. Abusers use cognitive distortions over and over again – like bad habits, which trap them into repeating the same mistakes. That is why it is so important to learn to recognize cognitive distortions – and to learn how to overcome them with clear *rational thinking*.

Unlike cognitive distortions, rational thinking is based on logic and correct information and a clear view of reality. "Irrational" means something is screwed up. It is not based on the truth or reality. Cognitive distortions are irrational.

cognitive distortions	=	irrational thoughts	=	cognitive distortions	=	thinking errors	=	automatic thoughts

Whatever we call them, the important thing is that cognitive distortions can be changed. The negativity that comes with cognitive distortions can be changed into positivity with rational thinking. Let's look at three cognitive distortions – and change them into rational thoughts:

Irrational thinking	Rational thinking
"I'm a total loser."	"I've got some problems, but I also have many strengths. I can make myself a better person."
"When I'm horny, I just can't stop myself."	"I always have some control – no matter how horny I feel."
"I want sex with her - so she must want sex with me."	"Nobody can read another person's mind. Just because I want sex doesn't mean that she does too."

The first step is learning to recognize negative thoughts and cognitive distortions when they occur. In this chapter, you'll be learning how to use that awareness and begin to change your negative thinking.

The basic idea is simple. It is not situations and events that cause our emotions and behavior. It is our thoughts about the situations that cause our emotions and behavior.

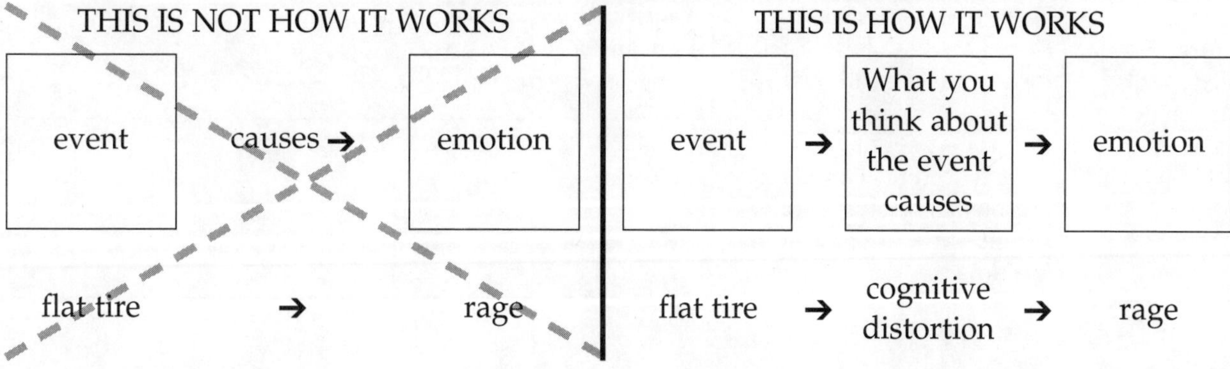

Negative thoughts lead to negative emotions and negative behavior. Positive thoughts lead to positive emotions and positive behavior. For example, if your car gets a flat tire, the flat tire is a negative event or trigger. It is your thinking about the flat tire that determines your emotional response and behavior.

If you have a cognitive distortion that getting a flat tire is a terrible disaster that will ruin your whole day, it will cause you to feel the emotion of rage and you are more likely to lose control of your behavior (such as scream and curse or bang your fist on the steering wheel).

But if you have the rational thought that getting a flat tire is just unlucky and is not so bad, you would feel the emotion of annoyance and keep your cool.

Trigger Event	Thinking	Emotional Reaction	Behavior	Outcome
Flat tire	Cognitive Distortion This is a disaster!	Rage	Slam your fist on the steering wheel and scream curses.	Bad
	Rational Thought This is an inconvenience.	Annoyance	Calmly get the car jack out of the trunk.	Good

Trigger Event	Thinking	Emotional Reaction	Behavior	Outcome
Another driver cuts in front of your car.	Cognitive Distortion That S.O.B. is disrespecting me. I'll teach him a lesson.	Rage	Scream curses and tailgate him in return, putting all the passengers in danger.	Bad
	Rational Thought That guy is driving like a jerk, but he doesn't know me from anybody.	Annoyance	Remain calm and allow the bad driver to pass.	Good

Trigger Event	Thinking	Emotional Reaction	Behavior	Outcome
See an attractive female at the mall.	Cognitive Distortion I want sex with her, so she must want sex with me.	Anger and sexual arousal	Follow her to the parking lot to harass her or rape her.	Bad
	Rational Thought Nobody can read another person's mind. Just because I want sex doesn't mean that she does too.	Attracted, but calm.	Continue shopping at the mall.	Good

In the next section, you will learn the basic method of (1) identifying cognitive distortions, (2) recognizing how they cause negative emotions and negative behavior, and then (3) how to change cognitive distortions into rational thinking that brings positive outcomes.

Using the Daily Record of Negative Thoughts

The Daily Record of Negative Thoughts on the following page is designed to help you figure out situations that cause you to feel or act in a way that is not in your best interest.

Situation (trigger event) – In the second column, briefly describe the event that caused you to have a negative emotion. Describe what happened as if a videotape would have recorded it. Sometimes it might be hard to identify a specific trigger. Negative emotions can occur as a result from being alone or just daydreaming about something. In this case, briefly describe the daydream or what you were thinking about just before the negative emotion.

Automatic thoughts (cognitive distortions) – Most people assume that it is a situation that causes an emotion. Actually, it is our thoughts about the situation that cause our emotions. In the third column, write down the thoughts that you had after the trigger event and before the emotion you felt. Sometimes it is easy for you to identify your thoughts. Sometimes they are harder to identify because they happen so quickly – as if they are "automatic." For these cases, you have to concentrate on what happened and your reaction to the event. Then write down the thought that comes to you. Then, rate how strongly you believe each "automatic thought" to be true, using a scale of 0 to 10 where 0 is the very least and 10 is the very most.

Emotions – Write down how you felt at the time in the fourth column. What emotion did you feel? Sadness, anger, depression, loneliness, fear, hopelessness? Emotions are different than your thoughts. Thoughts usually take the form of words, phrases, or sentences that we say to ourselves. It may take some practice to clearly see the difference between thoughts and emotions, but you will be able to do so. Then rate how strongly you felt the emotion, using a scale of 0 to 10.

Rational response – After you have written down your automatic thoughts, you need to question what is wrong with each thought. Is it correct? Do you know if it is a true fact or just someone's opinion? What is the evidence to prove or disprove the thought? Is there another way to look at the same event? Coming up with a rational response takes some practice. As you first begin learning how to do this, you may want to ask for help from the treatment staff or your primary therapist. After writing your rational response, then rate how strongly you believe the rational response to be true, using a scale of 0 to 10.

Outcome – After you have completed columns 1-4, rate how strongly you now believe the automatic thought in the second column, using a scale of 0 to 10. You will probably find that you do not believe the first idea as strongly as before.

Daily Record of Negative Thoughts Worksheet

DATE	SITUATION	AUTOMATIC THOUGHT (Cognitive distortion) Rate strength of belief from 0 to 10	EMOTION Rate strength of feeling from 0 to 10	RATIONAL RESPONSE Rate strength of belief from 0 to 10	OUTCOME Rate strength of belief in the automatic thought from 0 to 10

Daily Record of Negative Thoughts Worksheet

DATE	SITUATION	AUTOMATIC THOUGHT (Cognitive distortion) Rate strength of belief from 0 to 10	EMOTION Rate strength of feeling from 0 to 10	RATIONAL RESPONSE Rate strength of belief from 0 to 10	OUTCOME Rate strength of belief in the automatic thought from 0 to 10

Cognitive Distortions Exercise

Imagine that you have been in a group session for almost an hour. The room is hot and stuffy. People are spacing out and having trouble with paying attention. The topic is not very exciting. Some group members seem bored, some are annoyed, some are daydreaming. Finally the female counselor says, "That's it. It's too hot. Group is over. See you next time."

Read the automatic thoughts of each group member. For each automatic thought, mark an "X" for the ones that you might also think if you were in the group. Then go back through the list and mark an "X" to show whether the automatic thought is a rational thought or an irrational cognitive distortion.

Group member	Automatic Thoughts (cognitive distortions)	I might think that	Is it Rational?	Or Irrational?
A thinks:	This is all my fault. She's really mad at me for not paying attention.			
B thinks:	This is so stupid. I'm losing group time because other people are falling asleep. They are such jerks.			
C thinks:	Oh no. What if they give up on us and never call us back for group?			
D thinks:	Staff shouldn't act that way. They are supposed to help us and listen to us. They'll probably cancel class over and over now.			
E thinks:	It was hard to pay attention in that hot room. I hope it's cooler in there next time.			
F thinks:	I was doing alright. It's everyone else's fault. If they all weren't so lazy and stupid, everything would have been okay.			
G thinks:	I always thought staff cared about us and would do everything they could for us. Now I see they don't care about us at all.			

Group member	Automatic Thoughts (cognitive distortions)	I might think that	Is it Rational?	Or Irrational?
H thinks:	Great. She hates us. Now we'll have a super hard test when we get back and if I fail I'll get kicked out.			
I thinks:	I wasn't goofing off. I said the right answer. But now she will punish me too.			
J thinks:	If maintenance wasn't so lazy and fixed things, it wouldn't be so hot in here.			
K thinks:	I told her two times to call maintenance and get it fixed. What's wrong with these people?!			
L thinks:	I'm so stupid. I missed that question. I don't even know why I even try... I'll never learn all this stuff. I'm just dumb.			
M thinks:	Mr. X always ruins it for everybody. They should just throw him out of the program. Then we wouldn't have these problems anymore.			
N thinks:	This is great! Free afternoon.			
O thinks:	She's gonna get tired of this and stop giving us privileges. She's gonna put in my file that I wasn't learning anything. I'm gonna get punished.			
P thinks:	Dismissed? Forever? She is kicking us all out of group? I can't believe we all just got kicked out of the program.			
Q thinks:	If there's no group because it's too hot, then I guess that means we get the whole summer off.			
R thinks:	We will never get through this material. I'll be stuck here forever.			

If you want, you can use this space to make notes about what you learned from this lesson:

Controlling Anger By Changing Cognitive Distortions

How can you use rational thinking to get through a tense situation without losing control? One simple way is to remind yourself not to get upset. Remind yourself that you have the power to stay calm even if you are angry, and that by keeping calm gives you more power over the situation. In fact, you will usually feel less angry when you experience the feeling of having more control. Take a deep breath to help yourself relax. Then use clear thinking to understand what is happening and figure out what to do.

Here are some examples of rational thoughts that you could use to control anger in a tense situation:

- Getting upset will just make things worse.
- As long as I keep my cool, I'm in control.
- I can find a way to say what I want – without losing my temper.
- They might be expecting me to get angry. I'm going to show them I'm in control.
- I can manage this – I'm in control.
- I don't have to take this so seriously.
- I don't like what they're doing, but it's not unbearable. I can handle it okay.
- There's no point in getting mad.
- Instead of losing my temper, let me think of another way to handle this.

If none of the examples feels right for you, you should create your own rational response. If you have a rational response ready to use, it will help you keep control when you feel your anger rising.

Pick rational responses from the list that will work for you and write them below. Or make up some rational responses of your own. Write down a few rational responses that remind you to relax and will help you stay in control.

____

____

____

____

____

____

____

The Broken iPod™ Exercise

Instructions: You took your friend's iPod™ without asking him. You dropped it and broke it. He is very angry with you. Answer the following questions as if this real life event occurred to you.

What are my cognitive distortions when my friend is angry with me?	What emotions and behaviors occur when I have this cognitive distortion?	What are the consequences for me?
Examples: "It was a cheap player. Don't freak out at me!" "I always screw up. I'm just an idiot." "He'll think I did this on purpose!"		
What are the consequences for others?	What would be a more rational thought and better response?	What is the benefit to me for using a rational response?

Responsibility and Self-Management Skills

Intensive Treatment Phase

Level Two
Application

Responsibility and Self-Management Skills

Level II – Application begins with Chapter 4 on Abusing Others. This is where you begin to apply the knowledge about cognitive distortions and positive thinking that you learned in Chapters 1 to 3. The Abusing System shows how all of your thoughts, feelings and behaviors fit together in your abusive behavior.

In the Application level of the program, you will now begin to "apply" your new knowledge and gain even more knowledge and self-control as you go through the Resident Workbook and the treatment program. Some of the key areas in this level of the program include the following:

Chapter 4. Abuse System	• Learning how to change negative thinking into positive thinking. • Learning how various triggers, thoughts, feelings and beliefs combine to cause abusive behavior.
Chapter 5. Aggression System	• Learning how various triggers, thoughts, feelings and beliefs combine to cause aggressive urges and how they are related to abusive behavior.
Chapter 6. Beliefs: How It All Works Together.	• Learning how certain negative "core beliefs" about yourself and the world have a huge effect on how you think, feel and behave. • Beginning the process of changing negative core beliefs to create a healthy and positive sense of self-esteem and greater self-control.
Chapter 7. From Denial to Responsibility	• Learning how to really start taking responsibility for your abusive behavior and your future behavior.

Chapter 4
Abusive System

Abuse System Questions

In this section, you will answer a lot of questions about your own fantasies, thoughts, feelings and behaviors. Later, you will take your answers to each question and put them into an Abusive System Diagram, which will help you to see how all these pieces fit together to cause Abusive Behavior. If you can, try to answer the questions for one abusive act at a time.

Triggers – What kinds of situations and things cause you to start to have a thought, fantasy or feel an urge to abuse someone? (Some examples would be viewing pornography, getting drunk, going to a party, boredom, hanging around certain people and places, etc.). _______

____

____

____

____

____

Fantasies – If you have fantasies, what are your most frequent fantasies about abusing others? ____

____

____

____

____

____

Feelings – What feelings did you have when you abused? What other feelings go along with your fantasies and urges to abuse? ____________________________

Setting yourself up – What decisions did you make to "set yourself up" to abuse? What did you say to yourself to put yourself in a situation where you knew you were likely to abuse?

High risk situation – Describe the situation and place that made it easier or likely for you to abuse.

Beliefs at the time of the abuse – What did you believe about yourself, the victim or the situation that allowed you to make these bad decisions?

Your actions (behavior) – What actions did you take that put yourself into a situation where you were very likely to abuse?____

Your words (verbal behavior) – What did you say to set your victim up to be hurt or to set up the abuse? ____

Giving in to urges – When and why did you decide to give in to your thoughts and urges to abuse?____

Abusive behaviors – Briefly describe your abusive behaviors.____________________

Escaping responsibility – How did you escape from any guilt or bad feelings you may have had about hurting your victim? ____________________

Reliving the abuse through fantasy – Many abusers have fantasies. After the abuse, what parts of the abuse did you "relive" in your thoughts, fantasies and daydreams? ____________________

Denial – What did you think or tell yourself to pretend that you did not hurt your victim or to make yourself feel like you did not commit any serious abuse? ____________________

Recognizing Cognitive Distortions Used During Your Abuse

In the left column, write down the kinds of thoughts you had while you were setting up your abusive behavior or the thoughts you had while committing the abuse against a victim.

Thoughts Before and During Abuse	Type of Cognitive Distortion

Now, in the right column, write down what is wrong with each thought. What cognitive distortions did you use during your abuse? You can also use the list of cognitive distortions below (descriptions can be found in Chapter 2).

- All or nothing.
- Exaggerating.
- Seeing only the negative.
- Trashing the positive.
- Mind reading.
- How I feel is how it is.
- Blaming yourself.
- Blaming others.
- Making excuses.
- Minimizing.
- Poor me.

Rational Response Exercise

Use this chart to again write down your thoughts "during the abuse" (from previous page) and try to think of a clear rational correction for each cognitive distortion.

After you have made a rational response, rate how much you *believe* each new rational thought on a scale from 0 (least) to 10 (most).

My Thoughts During the Abuse	Rational Responses to Cognitive Distortions	Rating

How to Change Negative Thoughts and Feelings into Positive Ones

This is a way to help you deal with negative and painful emotions, such as loneliness, depression, anger, shyness, guilt, boredom, frustration, worry and fear. These are also the kinds of negative feelings and moods that can lead to abusive and other negative behavior. These negative feelings are not directly caused by negative events. They are caused by how you think about negative events. This is the key for changing negative, self-defeating thoughts (which cause rotten feelings) into positive thoughts and self-control (which create good feelings and self-pride).

There are five basic steps to this method:

(1) Describe the upsetting event ("trigger") – Write a brief description of the situation or problem that upset you in the left column.

(2) Identify your "automatic thoughts" following the trigger event – Record your first thoughts about the trigger event.

(3) Identify your negative feelings – Write down the negative emotions you feel and rate how much you are upset – from 0 (not upset at all) to 10 (the most upset I can be).

(4) Replace automatic thoughts with positive thoughts – In the column labeled "Rational Corrections" write down new rational ideas about the trigger event that are more positive and realistic.

(5) Outcome – Now that you have changed the negative thinking into positive thinking, rate how upset you now feel on the same scale from 0 (not upset at all) to 10 (the most upset I can be). You should find that rational thinking will greatly reduce how upset you feel. Sometimes it can even stop it.

Use the worksheet on the following page to practice.

Changing Negative Thoughts and Feelings into Positive Ones Worksheet (1)

Upsetting Event (trigger)	AUTOMATIC THOUGHTS	Emotional Reaction (rate from 0-10)	RATIONAL RESPONSES	Emotional Reaction (rate from 0-10)
Joe called me a "baby fag" in front of the group.	Now everyone will think I'm a "baby fag." No one will want to be my friend. I'm disgusting.	Rage – 9 Shame – 9	Just because someone calls me a name, doesn't make it true. No one even blinked an eye when Joe insulted me, so it looks like no one even cares what he said.	Anger – 2 Shame – 1

Changing Negative Thoughts and Feelings into Positive Ones Worksheet (2)

Upsetting Event (trigger)	AUTOMATIC THOUGHTS	Emotional Reaction (rate from 0-10)	RATIONAL RESPONSES	Emotional Reaction (rate from 0-10)

What to Do If You Still Believe Your Negative Thoughts

What happens if you tried to replace your negative thoughts (cognitive distortions) with positive thoughts (rational corrections), but you STILL believe the negative thoughts?

Don't panic. Don't feel ashamed. It happens. Remember that you're new at doing this. It takes practice to get better at something new. It's just like learning a sport or any other new skill. The more you practice, the easier it is to do and the better you get.

So, if you still believe in some of your negative thoughts, should you just keep quiet so no one knows? No. There is nothing wrong with getting stuck or trying to figure things out. It's very hard to change cognitive distortions. Sometimes it is very complicated. It often takes extra help and extra practice to catch on. This is where your primary therapist and other treatment staff can help you. Let them know when you're stuck or can't figure something out. Be honest that you still believe in the negative thoughts and need more help to change your cognitive distortions.

How to Use the Abusive Behavior System Diagrams

There are two Abusive Behavior System Diagrams on the next two pages. One is a blank copy for you to fill out and the other is already filled out to give you an example of someone else's abusive behavior system.

Please go back to your answers to the thirteen questions to the Abusive Behavior System Questions on pages IV-1 to IV-5. For each answer to the questions, you will find an empty box in the Abusive Behavior System Diagram. Read each answer and then cut it down to a few key words, which you can enter into each box in the diagram. For example, if your answer to question (1) was "watch a porno movie with a man raping a woman," you would write "watch rape porno" into box (1). If your answer to question (2) is "I fantasize about sneaking into my neighbor's bedroom and raping her," you would write "rape neighbor" into box (2). These are the thirteen boxes to fill out in the diagram.

(1) Triggers.
(2) Fantasies.
(3) Feelings.
(4) Setting yourself up.
(5) High risk situation.
(6) Beliefs at time of abuse.
(7) Your actions (behavior).
(8) Your words (verbal behavior).
(9) Giving in to urges.
(10) Abuse (or re-abuse).
(11) Escaping responsibility.
(12) Reliving the abuse through fantasy.
(13) Denial.

When you are done, take some time to look at the diagram. See how your triggers, fantasies, beliefs, feelings and behavior all fit together as one system. Think about it. What pattern do you see that you didn't see before? What have you learned about yourself?

Abusive Behavior System – Example

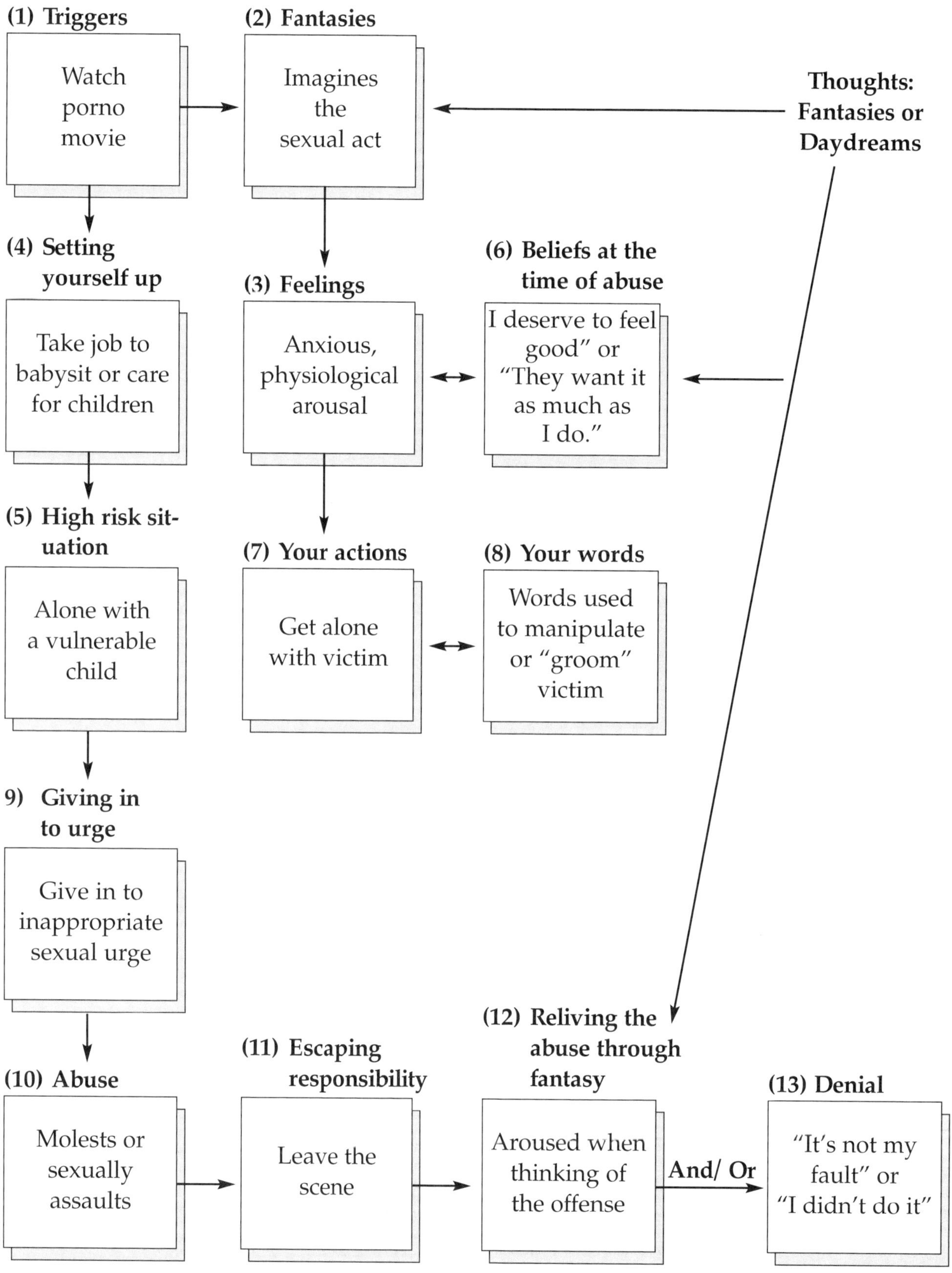

Abusive Behavior System

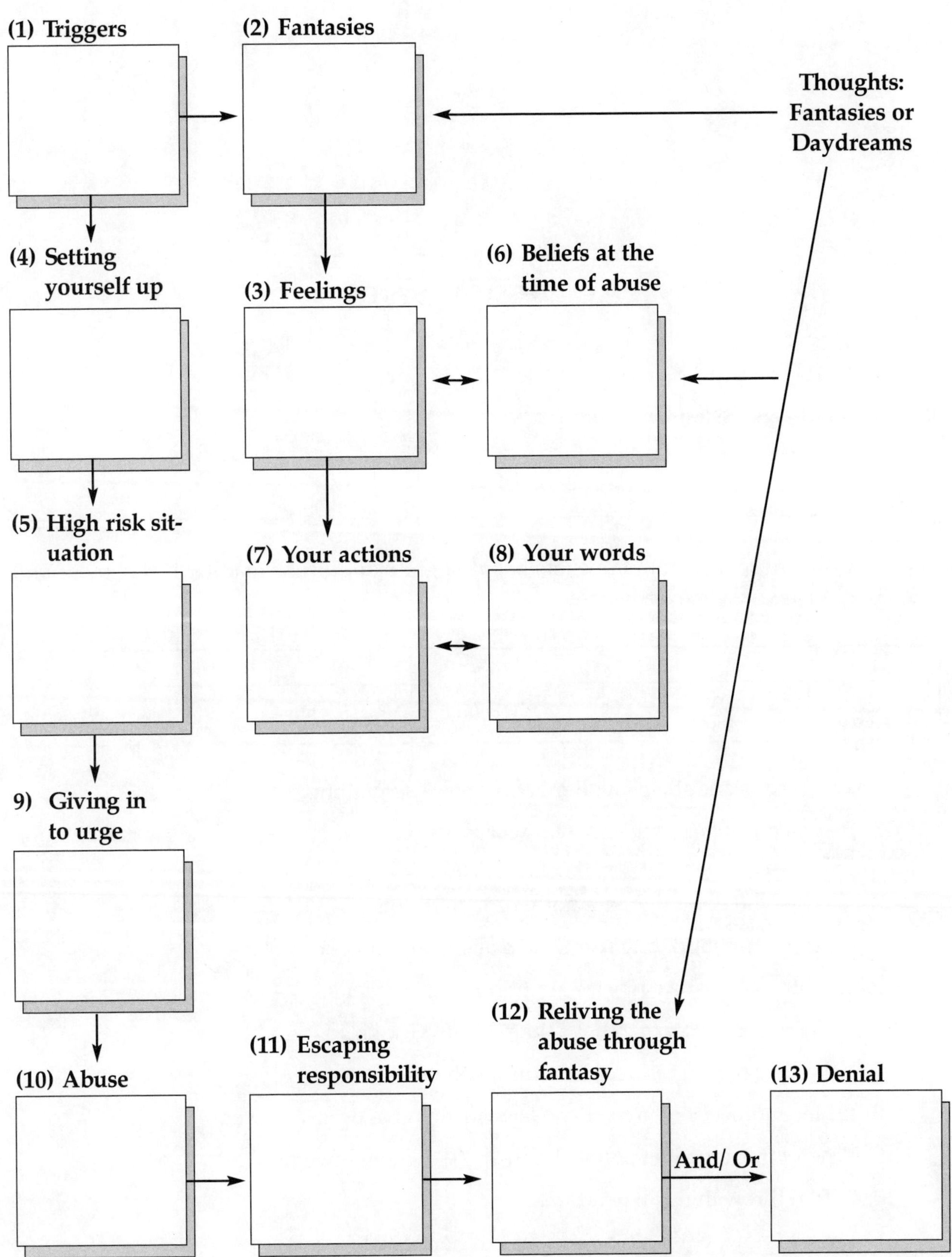

CHAPTER 5
AGGRESSION SYSTEM

Beliefs About Aggression Questions

Name: ______________________________ Date: ________________

Listed below are some common beliefs about aggression. Please read each statement and rate how much you agree or disagree.

1	2	3	4	5	6	7
Totally Disagree	Disagree Very Much	Disagree Slightly	Neutral	Agree Slightly	Agree Very Much	Totally Agree

____ 1. When someone shares with me, they want something.

____ 2. If someone disrespects me with words, its okay for me to physically attack him or her.

____ 3. People who don't fight are not worth anything.

____ 4. Scaring or intimidating someone makes me feel good.

____ 5. It's OK to think or fantasize about hurting someone.

____ 6. Some people deserve to have their "butts kicked."

____ 7. If another person teases me, I will get them.

____ 8. If I let another person have the last word, I give up my power.

____ 9. When I'm angry, I let people know it. "I let them have it."

____10. I often throw things when I'm angry.

____11. I don't know why I hit people, "it just happens."

1	2	3	4	5	6	7
Totally Disagree	Disagree Very Much	Disagree Slightly	Neutral	Agree Slightly	Agree Very Much	Totally Agree

____12. If I hurt someone who deserves it, "it is his or her fault."

____13. Hurting my victim wasn't my fault, it was because I was high or drunk.

____14. If I hurt my friends that bad, they wouldn't hang around me.

____15. Men should control women, it's our role in life.

____16. I was hit as a younger child, so I can't help being violent.

____17. The victim didn't do what I asked him/her, so that's why I hurt him/her.

____18. It was fun to make "a punk" out of that dude.

____19. Men should be able to handle themselves, so it's on him.

____20. My father beat me, it didn't hurt me.

____21. Only sissies or punks complain when they have been beaten.

____22. A good beating makes you strong.

____23. If I get that angry, then it's on them.

____24. Why would he say something to me, when he knows he'd get his butt kicked?

____25. Punks and women should keep their mouths shut and not start stuff.

How many of the statements did you agree with? Your opinions about these statements shows how you look at the world and the use of violence. These beliefs are based on your past history, your experiences and your belief system.

Exercise: It may be useful for you to go back through the list with your primary therapist (or this could be done in a group session with your peers) and talk about your experiences and beliefs and how they influenced your agreement and disagreement with the various statements.

Aggression and Violence Starts With Thinking

Aggression and violence starts with cognitive distortions and mistaken beliefs. Sometimes aggression happens so quickly that you can't believe that you had any thoughts at all before you acted in a violent way. But automatic thoughts can happen in a flash. Automatic thoughts can happen so fast that you may not even be aware of it.

Often people say things like, "I just got mad. It just happened. I got real angry and hit him." But it's not true. The truth is that *everything you do starts between your ears.*

Every action you do is based on a decision. It could be a decision to fight or not to fight; a decision to run or not to run; a decision to abuse or not to abuse someone; or a decision to participate in treatment or just daydream. All decisions are thoughts. Sometimes you decide in a flash; sometimes you decide after thinking about it for a long time.

You can learn to "freeze-frame" the times when you suddenly acted violently – those times when you were not even aware of having any thoughts. You'll see how certain beliefs and thinking can set you up to react badly, even violently. For example, you may have grown up in a home where you were often put down and yelled at. This may have led you to believe that you were a bad person and so you would expect to get yelled at. After that, you would be ready to snap back at the very first sign of trouble. That pattern becomes a habit, an "automatic" reaction that you're not even aware of.

Aggression can be slow or fast. "Slow" aggression is violence that you think about and plan ahead of time. This is aggression that you are ready and prepared to use. "Fast" aggression is violence that seems to happen in a split second. It seems like an instant reaction. *But, whether it's slow or fast, all aggression is driven by thinking.*

Think about a time recently when you lost your temper and acted aggressively. Did you act without thinking about it first? You're saying yes? Can you honestly say that you didn't think about it, even a little bit, before you did it?

Aggression and violence always serve a purpose for you. You may or may not be aware of what that purpose is, but it serves a purpose. Aggression and violence often begin with cognitive distortions and faulty beliefs. Take this example:

You're walking home and a man looks at you, and you think, "What's he want? What's his problem?" You give him a cold stare so he doesn't think that you're weak.

Here's what happens in a matter of seconds – in terms of cognitive distortions:

First cognitive distortion: ↓	"He wants to hurt me." ↓
Second cognitive distortion: ↓	"I have to get him first, or he'll think I'm weak." ↓
Your response (feelings and behavior):	Tense and fearful. "I'll give him the cold stare so he won't bother me."

Now, here's another fact about aggression and violence.

Extreme anger leads to more cognitive distortions.

In the same way, that cognitive distortions set you up to expect trouble and be ready to act violently, extreme emotions like anger and fear can fuel even more cognitive distortions that keep the ball rolling.

To use the example above:

First automatic thought: ↓	"He wants to hurt me." ↓
Second automatic thought: ↓	"I have to get him first, or he'll think I'm weak." ↓
Your response (feelings and behavior): ↓	Afraid and tense. "I'll give him the cold stare so he won't bother me." ↓
Fear fuels more cognitive distortions: ↓	"He looked back like he's gonna hit me." ↓
	"That S.O.B. thinks I'm weak. ↓
	"I won't be his bitch. I'll hit him first." ↓
	You attack him, knock him down and continue to punch him. ↓
	"You deserve this." "You're the punk now!" ↓
	The victim is seriously injured, but you don't feel any regret for attacking him without reasons. "He asked for it. That'll teach him to give me respect."

Write down some examples of the kinds of situations ("triggers") in which you easily lose your temper or act aggressively. Write down some of the thoughts that go along with the triggers and your reaction (feelings and behavior).

Triggers		Automatic Thought		Response (feelings and behavior)
	→		→	
	→		→	
	→		→	
	→		→	

Studying Your Anger

Think about some times when you felt rage and became violent. Then pick one time when you felt your most extreme rage and answer the following questions.

Describe the situation that made you so angry.____________________________

____

____

Did you try to threaten the other person before you became violent? What reaction did you get? ____

____

____

What were you thinking as you became more and more angry?__________________

____

____

How did other people react to you after seeing your rage? ___________________________

____

____

____

How did this experience change your feelings or your belief about yourself? ___________

____

____

____

System of Aggression Questions

The following questions will help you to understand your own System of Aggression. Your answers to each of the questions will later fit into a diagram of your individual System of Aggression and you will begin to gain the power and self-control to avoid falling into the same negative behaviors and violence.

Triggers – What is going on around you that makes you think about violence? Is there violence in your neighborhood? Do you watch a lot of violence on TV or videos. Do you play violent video games? Do you spend time on the computer in hateful, angry or violent web sites? ____

____

____

____

____

Negative thoughts – Think about the last time you were aggressive or violent toward someone. Write down your negative thoughts. For example, some of your negative thoughts may have included "getting even," "gaining respect", or "making the victim feel what you feel."

____

____

____

____

Beliefs about yourself – What did you believe about yourself that gave you a reason to attack or hurt the other person? For example, "I don't let anyone push me around" or "I'm really a coward" or "I have to be right or I'll look like an idiot." ______

______

______

______

______

Beliefs about the victim of violence – What did you believe about your victim that allowed you to be aggressive? What did you tell yourself about the victim that made it okay to be violent? ______

______

______

______

______

Feelings – In addition to anger and rage, what were your feelings just before you became aggressive? For example, other feelings could have been fear, shame, excitement, or hating yourself for not being able to control yourself. ______

______

______

______

______

Your actions – What actions did you take when you were violent? Describe how you chose the person you attacked? Describe what you did that hurt or harmed the other person. ___

______

______

______

______

Your words – What did you say or yell when you were aggressive? How did you use words or curse words to get control or have power to hurt the other person? ________________

____

____

____

____

Power and control issues – What things do you do to increase your feelings of power or control over other people? Examples could be starting fights, talking back, acting like a tough guy, having to always win, having to be in charge, or blaming other people for your own mistakes.____

____

____

____

Setting yourself up – What decisions do you make to set yourself up for violence? What decision do you make to place yourself in a position to be aggressive or violent? How did your decisions "put you in a box" and not allow you to walk away from a fight? Was getting respect or proving your manhood part of your decision or beliefs? ________________

____

____

____

High risk situation – Describe how you put yourself in a situation where it was likely to become violent. What was the high risk situation? ________________________

____

____

____

Giving in to the violent urge – What was the last chance that you had to walk away (and you didn't) before you decided to get violent? ________________________

____

____

____

The aggressive act – Describe the actual act of violence or aggression. What did you do?

____

____

____

____

Escape by blaming – How did you blame the other person for your violence? What did you say to yourself that let you escape responsibility for your violence? ______________

____

____

____

Relive the violence through fantasy – Do you continue to get some pleasure from remembering your violence or how it felt to terrify or control another person? Did thinking about violence make you feel powerful? ______________________________

____

____

____

Denial – What did you tell yourself to pretend that it was okay to be violent or that your violence did not seriously hurt your victim? For example, did you blame the victim for getting you angry and causing you to attack? ______________________________

____

____

____

Fake responsibility – How did you pretend to accept responsibility for your aggression in order to get out of trouble? ______________________________

____

____

____

Fake sorry – Did you pretend to feel sorry for causing harm with your violence? Did you say you felt bad for the victim of your violence? Did you apologize or write an apology in order to get out of trouble with the law or treatment providers? Did you fake sorry so you would look better? ____

____

____

____

____

How to Use the Aggression System Diagrams

There are two Aggression System diagrams on the next two pages. One is a blank copy for you to fill out and the other is already filled out to give you an example of someone else's aggression system.

In the next step, use a word or phrase that summarizes your response to each item from #1 to #17 and now enter it into the corresponding boxes in the "System of Aggression and Violence for Abusers" diagram on the next page. An example has been included to help you in completing your own personal diagram.

Please go back to your answers to the seventeen questions to the Aggression System Questions on pages VI-6 to VI-10. For each answer to the questions, you will find an empty box in the Aggression System Diagram. Read each answer and then cut it down to a few key words, which you can enter into each box in the diagram. For example, if your answer to question (1) was "Someone insulted me," you would write "Someone insulted me" into box (1). These are the seventeen boxes to fill out in the diagram.

(1) Triggers.
(2) Negative thoughts.
(3) Beliefs about yourself.
(4) Beliefs about victim of violence.
(5) Feelings.
(6) Your actions.
(7) Your words.
(8) Power, and control issues.
(9) Setting yourself up.
(10) High risk situation.
(11) Giving in to the violent urge.
(12) The aggressive act.
(13) Escape by blaming.
(14) Relive the violence through fantasy.
(15) Denial.
(16) Fake responsibility.
(17) Fake sorry.

When you are done, take some time to look at the diagram. See how your triggers, fantasies, beliefs, feelings and behavior all fit together as one system. Think about it. What pattern do you see about your aggressiveness that you didn't see before? What have you learned about yourself?

Aggregation System – Example

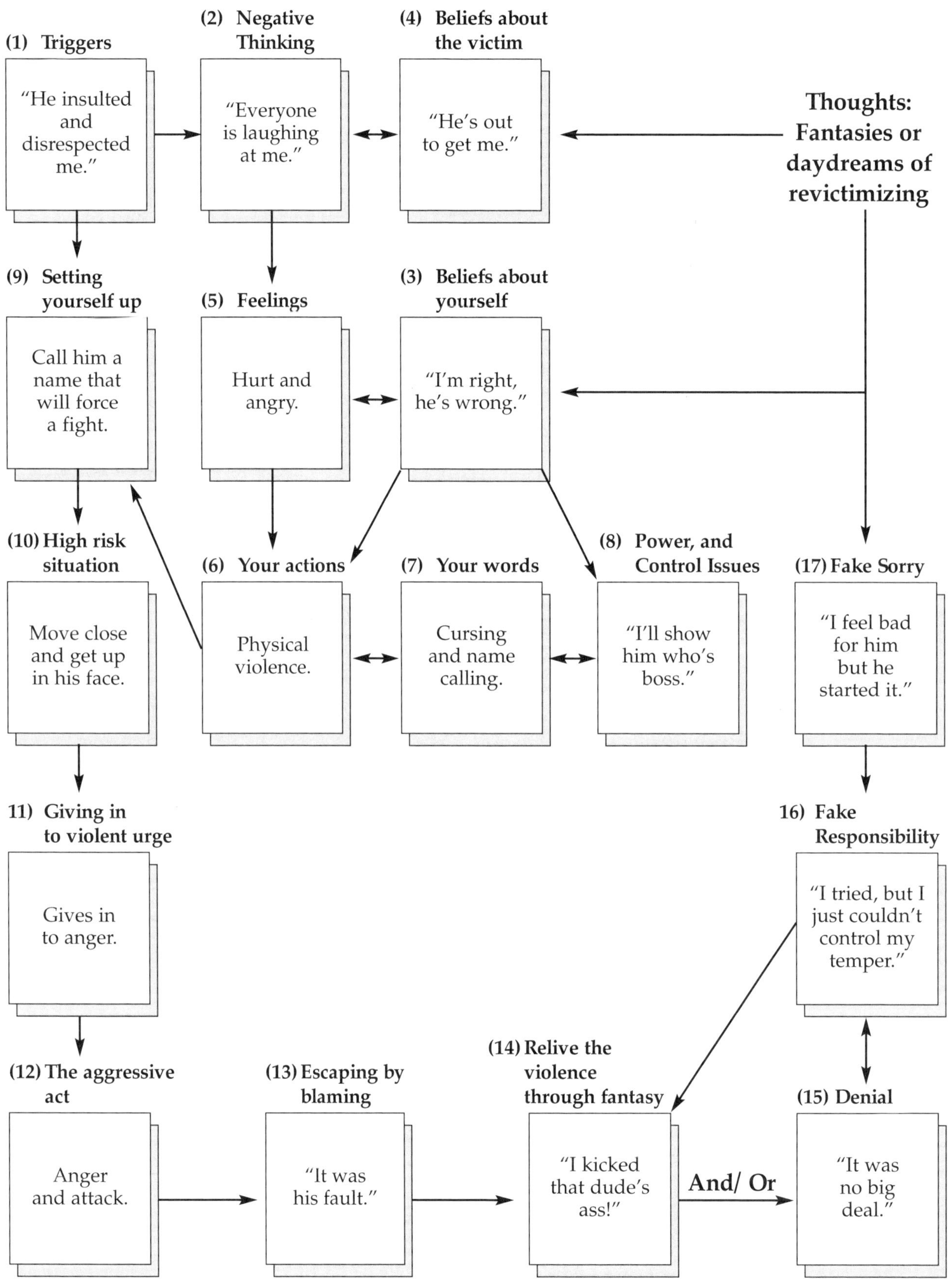

Aggregation System

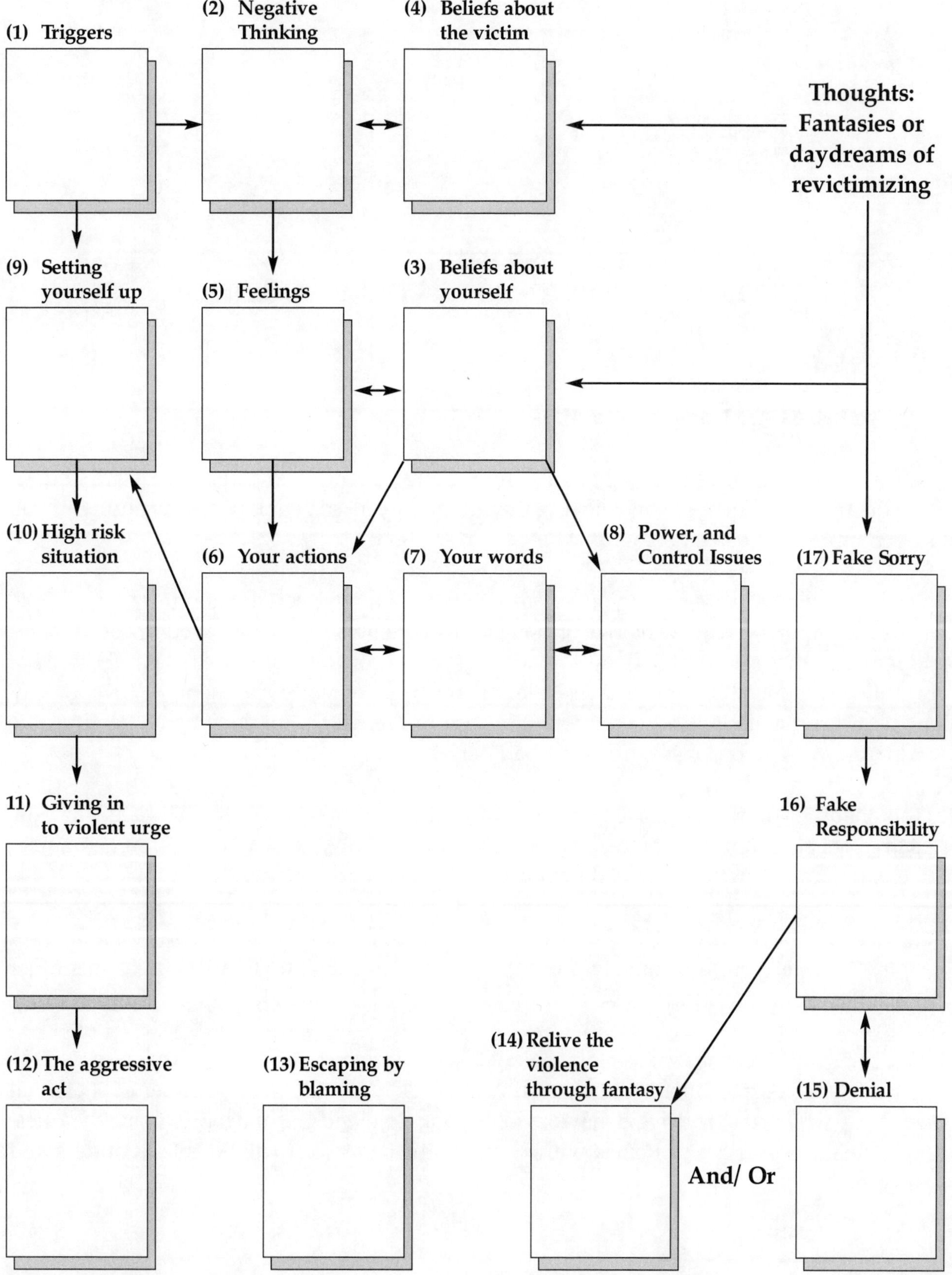

Chapter 6
Beliefs – How It All Works Together

Negative Beliefs Are Connected to Abuse

There are many negative beliefs that are connected to violence and abuse. Many are so deep that you are not even aware of believing them. But they all play a part in how and why you have committed abusive behavior.

Some of these beliefs are about yourself as a person, whether you are good or bad, competent or incompetent, worthy of love or not. Some are beliefs about your victim, about males and females, about sex and sexuality, about power and control. Some are beliefs about what you think you "need" or must have – like the need for sex, or excitement, or love, or violence. And some are beliefs about your purpose in life, your morals, where you fit in the world, and who is responsible for your bad behavior.

In this chapter, you will be learning more about "negative beliefs." You will be learning how negative beliefs can make you feel bad about yourself, how they can make you act in negative ways, and how they can lead to abusive behavior and violence.

Your negative beliefs – what you believe about yourself, your victim, the world, and other people – can get you in trouble by giving yourself "permission" to abuse and hurt other people. But if you can *change* these same negative beliefs, it can help stop you from abusing again.

The next series of questions will help you uncover some of the many different beliefs that played a part in your abusive behavior. Take your time and think deeply about the questions. The more you can be honest with yourself, the better you will be able to understand yourself.

Before the abuse: Start this exercise by closing your eyes and trying to picture yourself in the time and place just before you committed the abuse. Take a moment to remember. Where were you? Who were you with? What were you doing? How were you feeling? What were you thinking about? What was on your mind then? What was the last thought you had before you committed the abuse? Write down the thoughts, ideas and beliefs you had before the abuse. ______________________________

____

____

____

____

Beliefs about the victim before the abuse: Most abusers have negative beliefs that give themselves permission to abuse their victims. They often have beliefs that make the victim seem less human. This happens with pornography too. The people in pornography are not seen as real people. They are seen only as sex objects – things that arouse sexual desire. The same thing happens in abuse. The abuser does not see the victim as a real person. The victim is nothing more than an object that is the target or can fulfill his urge or desire. For example, an abuser might tell himself that his victim is "just a rich bastard," or "just another junkie," or "she does it with everyone else."

How did your beliefs allow you to turn your victim into an object? How did your beliefs turn your victim into someone less human or someone who does not deserve respect or compassion? Write down the beliefs that you are aware of. ______________________________

____

____

____

____

____

Beliefs immediately after the abuse: Now close your eyes and try to picture yourself in the time and place just after you abused. What were you doing? How were you feeling? What were you thinking about? What did you think about the victim? Write down the thoughts, ideas and beliefs you had immediately after the abuse. ______________________________

____

____

____

Today: What do believe about the abuse today? How do you feel when you remember it? What did you think about the victim today? What is different now? Write down the thoughts, ideas and beliefs you have today about the abuse.

Some Negative Beliefs of Abusers

Here is a list of some common beliefs that abusers have about themselves and the world. Make a mark beside the beliefs that you agree with.

"It's all about me"

- I take what I want.
- It's owed to me, I should have it.
- If anyone tries to keep me from what I want, then he/she is against me or he/she is not being fair.
- People should see it my way.
- If I want something or want to avoid something, then it justifies my actions.
- If I have a reason, I can make it "all right."

"Thinking is believing"

- If I have a thought and feeling, it must be true. If I think so, it must be so.
- If I want something to happen, it should.
- If things don't go the way I think they should, it's terrible.

Feelings make facts

- I know I'm right because I feel right about it.
- I should be happy all the time. Unhappiness is caused by other people and situations that I have no control over.

Avoidance

- If I don't think about a problem, it will go away.
- It's easier to avoid problems and responsibilities than to face them.

Other people aren't important

- Other people don't matter unless they can directly control things that I want.
- People are only important based on what they can do to me or for me.

The past determines my present

- The things that happened to me as a kid make me the way I am today. I can't do anything about it.
- I am what I am.
- I can't change the way I think.
- I can't change what happened to me. This is the only way I know how to be.

I must be in control

- Strong people don't ever need to ask for help.
- I can solve my own problems if I try hard enough.

Strong people don't show their feelings

- I never let other people know how I feel.
- If you cry or show feelings, it proves you're weak.
- If people find out that you are weak, they will laugh at you and use you.

If there's no proof...

- If you don't see it or hear it, it doesn't count.
- I won't accept responsibility for something you can't prove I did.
- Out of sight, out of mind.
- If you don't know about it, why should I tell you?

Who cares?

- No one else cares, so why should I?
- My best isn't good enough.
- Consequences really don't matter.
- Nothing goes right for me anyhow.

Look back over the beliefs that you agreed with. What pattern do you see? Which belief do you believe most strongly of all? Why?

____

____

____

____

Beliefs About Myself

1. Who are you? Describe yourself as a person. Describe your physical appearance. What do you believe you look like to others? ____

____

____

____

2. Describe how you act and interact with other people. What is your personality like?

____

____

____

____

3. Describe the true person you believe you are inside. If you think that no one knows the real you, now's your chance. What is inside the person that other people see as just an abuser? Describe the person inside that only you know.______________________________

____

____

____

____

____

4 Do you believe that anyone truly loves you? If so, who? ______________________

____

5. Do you believe you are worthy of love?______________________________________

6. Do you believe that you push people away from you? Why? ____________________

____

____

____

____

7. Do you feel like you are not worthy or good enough as a person? When, where, why?

8. Do you believe in God or a higher power? How would you describe it?

9. Do you believe a set of morals that say what is right and wrong? Describe it.

10. Does your belief about yourself change from situation to situation or from time to time? Do you feel better about yourself in particular situations, with particular people, or during particular activities? Do you see a change in your belief when you feel good in different situations? What's the difference?

11. Describe how your self-pride is connected to things you own or have. What things make you feel proud of yourself? A nice car? Money? Clothes? Friends? What things do you want just to show off? Is there something that you are proud of, but you believe that other people won't care or will laugh at you?

12. Do you think that you can change any of your beliefs? Why?

Beliefs About Control

Please read each of the following beliefs. Then, use the scale from 1 to 9 to show how strongly you agree or disagree with each belief If you don't know, mark "5" to show that you can't decide or that you both agree and disagree.

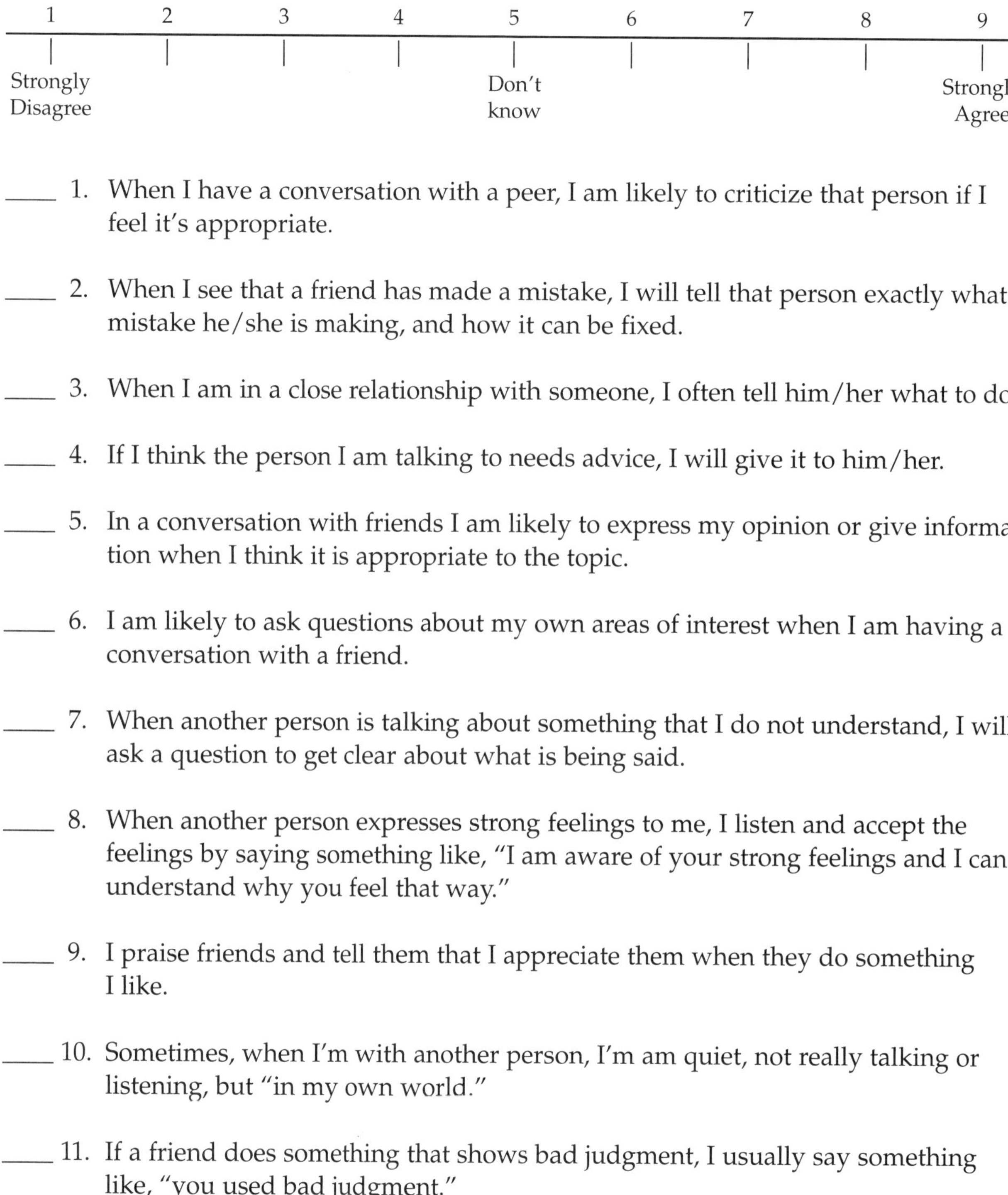

1	2	3	4	5	6	7	8	9
Strongly Disagree				Don't know				Strongly Agree

____ 1. When I have a conversation with a peer, I am likely to criticize that person if I feel it's appropriate.

____ 2. When I see that a friend has made a mistake, I will tell that person exactly what mistake he/she is making, and how it can be fixed.

____ 3. When I am in a close relationship with someone, I often tell him/her what to do.

____ 4. If I think the person I am talking to needs advice, I will give it to him/her.

____ 5. In a conversation with friends I am likely to express my opinion or give information when I think it is appropriate to the topic.

____ 6. I am likely to ask questions about my own areas of interest when I am having a conversation with a friend.

____ 7. When another person is talking about something that I do not understand, I will ask a question to get clear about what is being said.

____ 8. When another person expresses strong feelings to me, I listen and accept the feelings by saying something like, "I am aware of your strong feelings and I can understand why you feel that way."

____ 9. I praise friends and tell them that I appreciate them when they do something I like.

____ 10. Sometimes, when I'm with another person, I'm am quiet, not really talking or listening, but "in my own world."

____ 11. If a friend does something that shows bad judgment, I usually say something like, "you used bad judgment."

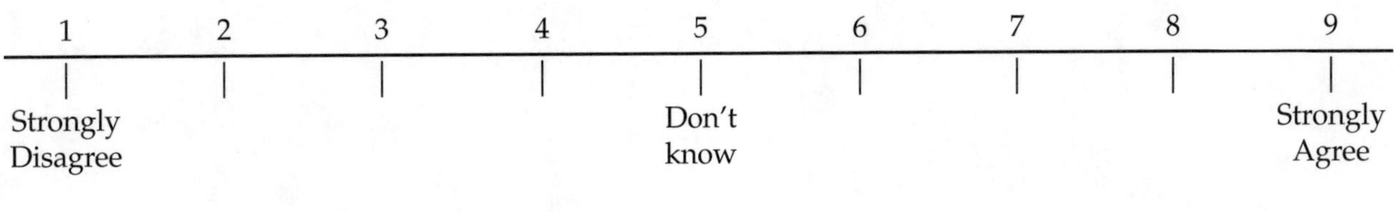

____ 12. If I see a co-worker making an error, I will tell the person what I think and explain how it could be fixed.

____ 13. If I want someone I'm with to do something, I am likely to tell him/her to do it.

____ 14. I freely give advice to other people.

____ 15. When talking to another person, I often express my opinion and provide information about the topic under discussion.

____ 16. In conversations with friends, I think of questions to ask them.

____ 17. When I am listening to another person, I check my understanding by asking questions.

____ 18. I can accept statements that other people make even if I disagree.

____ 19. In a relationship, I respond very positively to the other person.

____ 20. When I am with a member of my family, I often just sit and think.

____ 21. There are times when I criticize or speak sarcastically to another person.

____ 22. If a member of my family has problems or makes mistakes, I will tell that person how to fix it.

____ 23. I give directions to friends when I think they need to be told what to do.

____ 24. I make suggestions to people if I think they need to hear my point of view.

____ 25. I give my opinion or present facts easily when talking to others.

____ 26. When I'm talking with a peer, I ask questions based on my own interests.

____ 27. If a friend is telling me something, I will make it clear by asking him/her questions.

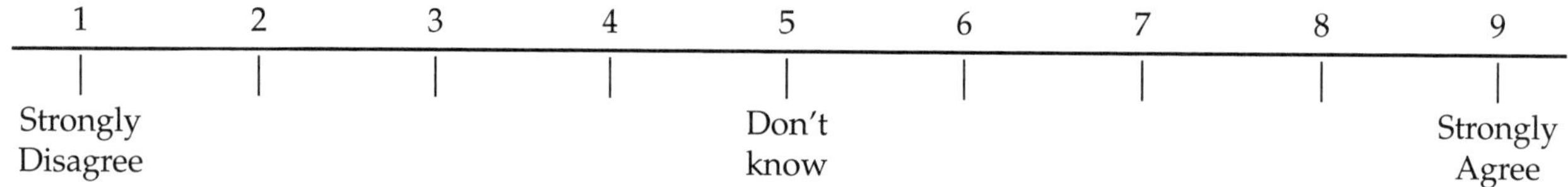

____ 28. When I'm talking in a conversation, I typically listen and acknowledge what I hear.

____ 29. It is quite common for me to praise and approve of comments I hear others make.

____ 30. When I'm with another person, we spend the time by sitting silently, not talking to one another.

Beliefs About Closeness

Name: ____ Date:____________________

Imagine yourself with another person or persons that you trust or feel close to. Then read each question and mark an "X" for the statement that best matches your behavior.

1. When I am thinking about how to start the conversation, I would probably:
   [ ] a. say nothing, just listen (1)
   [ ] b. tell how I feel (10)
   [ ] c. relate my feelings in other situations (7)
   [ ] d. ask people to relate what they know about groups in general (3)

2. If I am talking about goals, I would probably
   [ ] a. say that everyone needs goals (3)
   [ ] b. share what I see happening in the relationship (9)
   [ ] c. remind the other person of a previous time when the same subject was discussed (6)
   [ ] d. express my feelings about not having a goal (10)

3. When I am worried about somebody who is close to me (or my group), I would probably
   [ ] a. express some psychological theory (3)
   [ ] b. express my feelings to people in a different group to which I belong (7)
   [ ] c. express my feelings toward the person(s) who I am with now (10)
   [ ] d. change the subject (2)

4. If authority was an issue in my relationship, I would probably
   [ ] a. express my feelings about another group I belong to (7)
   [ ] b. say something about the role of person(s) I am with (9)
   [ ] c. express my feelings toward authorities I have known (7)
   [ ] d. bring up similar events from past discussions (6)

5. If the topic deals with reactions to strong emotions, I would probably
   [ ] a. tell how I feel when I am with other friends (7)
   [ ] b. tell how I feel toward the person with whom I am talking (10)
   [ ] c. start discussing emotions in relationships and groups (3)
   [ ] d. change the topic (2)

6. If the topic is about sex, I would probably
    [ ] a. talk about how people deal with the topic of sex (3)
    [ ] b. express my feelings to those I am with (10)
    [ ] c. talk about my feelings about sex in other relationships (7)
    [ ] d. remind the person(s) of a discussion on the same topic in the past (6)

7. If the conversation seems to have a violent tone, I would probably
    [ ] a. tell how I am feeling (10)
    [ ] b. point out that violence is part of all groups (3)
    [ ] c. talk about conflicts I have fixed in the past (6)
    [ ] d. say nothing and hope the subject changes (1)

8. If I am talking about some activities I could do with another person, I would probably
    [ ] a. say that I wish I could express my feelings (8)
    [ ] b. express my feelings about the activities (10)
    [ ] c. relate how people use activities to meet the need of getting closer (3)
    [ ] d. tell how I share confidences with others (4)

9. In a period of uncomfortable silence, I would probably
    [ ] a. wait to hear how the other person(s) reacts (1)
    [ ] b. express my feelings about the silence (10)
    [ ] c. share my observations about what's happening in the situation (9)
    [ ] d. say that the group has had periods of silence in the past (6)

10. If I am talking about how close I want to be to another person, I would probably
    [ ] a. tell how I feel about getting close to the other person (10)
    [ ] b. say that I have decided to sit quietly (9)
    [ ] c. tell how I feel about being close to other persons (7)
    [ ] d. say that I have discussed this issue with another person (4)

11. If I am talking about the weather, I would probably
    [ ] a. continue the discussion (2)
    [ ] b. tell how I feel about the discussion (10)
    [ ] c. tell how I think the weather affects my relationship (9)
    [ ] d. tell how the weather influences my feelings toward my (other) friends (7)

12. If I seem to be avoiding an important issue, I would probably
    [ ] a. talk about the tendency of people to avoid painful issues (3)
    [ ] b. make an observation about the present situation (9)
    [ ] c. tell how I deal with difficult issues with my (other) friends (7)
    [ ] d. express my feelings about the discussion (10)

13. If the person I am with has just told me that he/she is attracted to me, I would probably
    [ ] a. express my feelings at that moment (10)
    [ ] b. talk about interpersonal attraction (3)
    [ ] c. say that he/she seems to feel free to express feelings (9)
    [ ] d. tell about feelings I have had toward others (7)

14. If I am talking about fears of being hurt in a relationship, I would probably
    [ ] a. talk about fear in groups (3)
    [ ] b. relate times this has occurred before in this relationship (6)
    [ ] c. talk about my feelings about being hurt by others (7)
    [ ] d. describe how I have dealt with this with other friends (4)

15. If I am talking about leaders, I would probably
    [ ] a. change the subject of the discussion (2)
    [ ] b. say that I must find my own direction (9)
    [ ] c. describe my relationship with an authority figure in my life (4)
    [ ] d. state my feelings about leaders with whom I interact (7)

16. If I am talking about relationships, I would probably
    [ ] a. tell about feelings I have for someone close to me (7)
    [ ] b. describe some of my other relationships (4)
    [ ] c. tell what I see happening in this relationship (9)
    [ ] d. express my feelings about leaders with whom I interact (7)

17. If I have been talking about the weather, I would probably
    [ ] a. wait for a more interesting topic (1)
    [ ] b. state that this topic seems to come up often (6)
    [ ] c. talk about what my family does in this weather (4)
    [ ] d. comment on the behavior of the person I am with (9)

18. If the person I am with seems angry at me, I would probably
    [ ] a. remind him/her about the positive aspects of our relationship (8)
    [ ] b. tell what I know about scape-goating (3)
    [ ] c. talk about the increasing tension in all areas of society (3)
    [ ] d. tell how the anger makes me feel (10)

19. If I am talking about being close, I would probably
    [ ] a. change the subject (2)
    [ ] b. talk about what I and another person have talked about (4)
    [ ] c. talk about a time in the past when I have felt close to the others (6)
    [ ] d. tell about the feelings I am having presently (10)

20. If I am talking about comfort in relationships, I would probably
    [ ] a. suggest an activity (2)
    [ ] b. talk about comfort needs that people feel (3)
    [ ] c. share my feelings about the discussion (10)
    [ ] d. share how I feel when I are with my family (7)

21. If I am talking about intimate relationships, I would probably
    [ ] a. talk about limits in relationships (3)
    [ ] b. discuss limits I set in my other relationships (4)
    [ ] c. sit quietly and listen (1)
    [ ] d. tell what I am feeling now (10)

22. If the conversation lags, I would probably
    [ ] a. start some "small talk" (2)
    [ ] b. say that I would like to talk (8)
    [ ] c. make an observation on the situation (9)
    [ ] d. ask if the other person is uncomfortable with the situation (8)

23. If the other person is angry at me for talking too much, I would probably
    [ ] a. say that he/she seems angry (0)
    [ ] b. express my feelings about the person's anger (10)
    [ ] c. tell about people I know who talk a great deal (4)
    [ ] d. say that groups always have talkers and non-talkers (3)

24. If I am arguing about politics, I would probably
    [ ] a. express my feelings about the conflict (9)
    [ ] b. continue the discussion (3)
    [ ] c. relate how I have felt about similar arguments with others (7)
    [ ] d. describe a discussion I had with (other) friends on the same subject (4)

25. If I am involved in intense conflict, I would probably
    [ ] a. talk about how I feel (10)
    [ ] b. talk about conflicts and intimacy in relationships and groups (9)
    [ ] c. state that I am aware of the conflict (9)
    [ ] d. listen to see how the other person(s) feel(s) (1)

26. When I have been bored by the conversation for about five minutes, I would probably
    [ ] a. say how I feel (10)
    [ ] b. say I'd like to talk about something else (8)
    [ ] c. talk about my job (4)
    [ ]d. sit quietly and wait for a topic I like (1)

27. If the topic is sex, I would probably
   [ ] a. express my feelings toward the other(s) (10)
   [ ] b. tell what I know of sexual behavior (3)
   [ ] c. describe the present interaction (9)
   [ ] d. change the subject (2)

28. If I am about to leave, I would probably
   [ ] a. tell what I will be doing later (4)
   [ ] b. talk about some important events of the conversation (9)
   [ ] c. tell how I feel about having to leave (10)
   [ ] d. talk about how people say goodbye (3)

29. If I am talking about intimacy, I would probably
   [ ] a. tell how I feel about the other(s) (10)
   [ ] b. express what I think I should do to be closer (8)
   [ ] c. tell the person how he/she affects my life (9)
   [ ] d. talk about how I feel about similar situations with others in my life (7)

30. If I am trying to evaluate my relationship, I would probably
   [ ] a. talk about various ways to judge a relationship (3)
   [ ] b. ask the other person for a reaction (8)
   [ ] c. express my feelings about the relationship (10)
   [ ] d. talk about my observations of this relationship in the past (6)

Types of Beliefs Used by Abusers

There are different kinds of beliefs that an abuser can have to make it "seem" okay to abuse others. Some are beliefs about himself as a person; some are beliefs about what he thinks he must have; some are beliefs about why he abused.

CORE BELIEFS: These are deep-set beliefs that an abuser has about himself, which define who he is as a person. Core beliefs have an impact on how a person thinks, feels, and behaves day to day.

Example: "I am a bad person and I don't deserve to feel good."

Write a negative core belief about yourself. ______________________________

____

____

____

____

EXPECTATIONS: These are beliefs about what the abuser expects to gain from the abuse. It may be expectations of a "thrill" or "excitement" or "showing off."

Example: "Everyone will think I'm cool if I steal this car."

Write something you expected to gain from the inappropriate behavior. ____________

____

____

____

____

SELFISH "NEEDS": Abusers often tell themselves that they "need" or "deserve" or "must have" something – by abusing. These beliefs are totally selfish and distort the truth. No one ever needs or deserves something so badly that he has the right to hurt other people to get what he wants. Selfish beliefs show no regard for the needs of the victim.

Example: "I want those chains right now!"

Write a selfish need belief you have had about "needing" something from a victim. ______

____

____

____

____

GREEN LIGHTS: "Green light" beliefs give the abuser the permission to go ahead with the abuse. They are beliefs that the abuser uses to tell himself its okay to commit the abuse. For example, it could be the belief that no one will ever find out, or that he can get away with the abuse without being punished, or that the victim really wants sex from him.

Example: "He's so rich, he can just get another one."

Write a "green light" belief you used to go forward with an abuse. ________________

____

____

____

____

NOT MY FAULT: These beliefs help the abuser to deny responsibility for the abuse. They put the responsibility for the abuse on the victim, or other people, or the situation. "It's not my fault, I was drunk." "He started the fight." "I was too high to think straight." "She's asking for it if she dresses that way." These beliefs tell the abuser that he is not really responsible for his behavior.

Example: "He disrespected me. So he got what he deserved."

Write a "not my fault" belief you have used to deny responsibility for your abuse.

____

____

____

____

JUSTIFICATION: Justification beliefs don't even admit that the abuse was bad or harmful. They try to give the appearance that there was a "good reason" for the abuse. Justification beliefs try to "justify" the abuse. Justification beliefs are often mixed with "not my fault" beliefs. Both try to make excuses and avoid any responsibility for causing harm to another person. Justification beliefs usually happen before the abuse and allow the abusive behavior to occur and re-occur. Later, during treatment, these beliefs block abusers from taking responsibility and having empathy for victims.

Example: "Stealing cars doesn't hurt anybody. The insurance company just pays for another car."

Write a belief you used to make it look like you had a "good reason" for acting out.

____

____

____

____

____

Belief Pattern Worksheet

Take your written answers from the preceding exercise and insert them into this chart.

Core belief: "I'm a weak person." ↓	CORE BELIEF ↓
Expectation: "Beating him up will make me feel powerful." ↓	EXPECTATION BELIEF ↓
Selfish needs: "I want that right now." ↓	SELFISH "NEEDS" BELIEF ↓
Green Light: "The keys are in the ignition." ↓	"GREEN LIGHT" BELIEF ↓
Not my fault: "I was high." ↓	"NOT MY FAULT" BELIEF ↓
Justification: "He was asking for trouble." ↓	JUSTIFICATION BELIEF ↓

Now look for a pattern in the beliefs you wrote down. In what ways do your negative beliefs feed each other? How does one belief support the next belief? How do they "add up" to create abusive attitudes and behavior? ______________________________

____

____

____

____

____

How to Change Negative Beliefs

Negative core beliefs can have a lot of power to make a person feel badly and act badly. But, even though you may have some negative core beliefs, it is in your power to change them. By changing these negative beliefs, you can begin to feel better about yourself and gain better control over your life.

One way to change negative beliefs is to "put them to the test." You can learn to challenge the truth of a belief by getting evidence that helps to prove or disprove it.

For example, "Doug" believed that, "I'm just too ugly to love." Doug wasn't really ugly. But he believed he was ugly. Doug did not dare to ask someone for a date because he believed he would be rejected for being ugly.

Doug was given the assignment of getting "evidence" to prove or disprove his belief that he was ugly. He went out and asked different people for their opinion on his appearance. He was happy to find that no one viewed him as ugly. But he did get some good advice to get a better-looking haircut and clothes.

Now it's your turn to try the same method of changing negative beliefs about yourself. Begin by writing down one negative belief about yourself that you really believe is true. It should be a belief that is important to you – a belief that has a big effect on your view of yourself or the world.

CORE BELIEF ABOUT MYSELF:____

____

____

____

Now, take a minute to consider that negative belief. What would be a different way of looking at it? What is the very opposite of the negative belief? Could that be true? What is a more positive alternative belief?

For example, Doug believed that "I'm too ugly to love." A different, more positive belief could be: "I'm not handsome, but I'm decent looking." OR "Maybe I could look good if I got a haircut and dressed better." OR "Maybe I haven't had much luck in finding love yet, but it doesn't mean I'm not worthy of love."

Now write down some new positive alternatives to your own negative belief. Write down a different idea that could also be possible.

POSSIBLE ALTERNATIVE POSITIVE BELIEF: ____________________

____

____

____

____

Now put both beliefs to the test. Think about what evidence you can find that supports the negative belief. Write the evidence down. Think about what evidence you could find that supports the alternative positive belief. Write that evidence down.

Then consider the evidence supporting each belief. Rate how strongly you now believe the negative and the positive belief. Rate the strength of each belief from 1 (very weak) to 10 (very strong).

Write down evidence that supports the NEGATIVE CORE BELIEF	Write down evidence that supports the ALTERNATIVE POSITIVE BELIEF
Rate belief in the negative core belief from 1 to 10: ____________	Rate belief in alternative positive belief from 1 to 10: ____________

Reducing the Strength of Negative Core Beliefs

Here is more practice at changing negative beliefs. In the left column, write down some of the "core beliefs" that you have recognized in yourself. Then rate the strength of each belief from 1 (very weak) to 10 (very strong). Then come up with a rational alternative belief and rate the strength of your belief in the alternative positive belief.

NEGATIVE CORE BELIEF	RATE BELIEF	TYPE OF COGNITIVE DISTORTION	ALTERNATIVE POSITIVE BELIEF	RATE BELIEF
Example: I'm a bad person and I don't deserve to feel good.	9	All or nothing Blaming self	I'm not perfect. No one is. But sometimes I can be a good person.	6

Feeling, Belief, Thought Worksheet

In this exercise, you'll start with negative feelings and then look for the underlying negative core beliefs that may be causing the negative feelings. In the left column, enter a negative emotion that you are feeling now, or a negative emotion that you often feel (e.g., depressed, angry, lonely, fearful, etc.). Then consider what negative core belief may be creating that feeling. Write the negative belief in the middle column and then write down examples of the negative thoughts that seem to "automatically" come from the negative belief in the right column.

FEELING	NEGATIVE BELIEF	AUTOMATIC THOUGHTS THAT COME FROM NEGATIVE BELIEF
Unloved	"If people get to know me they will think I'm a loser. But if I impress them, they will like me."	"She doesn't like me. I'll be rejected." "I'm boring." "If I act nasty first, they can't reject me."
Helpless	"I am stupid and incompetent. I always need someone with me to help me."	"I can never learn this stuff. I give up." "Screw it, why bother." "I always need somebody to help me to do things right. I look like a crybaby."

Changing Negative Beliefs Worksheet

Write down some negative beliefs that you used on the Feeling, Belief, Thought Worksheet. Rate the strength of each negative belief from 1 (very weak) to 10 (very strong). Then come up with an alternative positive belief. Rate the strength of your belief in the alternative belief.

NEGATIVE CORE BELIEF	RATE BELIEF	NEW POSITIVE BELIEF	RATE BELIEF

From Seeing to Believing Worksheet

How you see things is shaped by your inside beliefs… which shape your thoughts. Deep-set negative beliefs can cause you to see things in negative ways. The way you see things is shaped by what you believe, and what you believe is based on your past experience. You can't change your past experiences, but you can change your beliefs.

Beliefs are powerful. They can rule your thoughts, feelings and behavior. You can try to change your negative thinking, but if you don't change your underlying negative core beliefs, your old habits of cognitive distortion will sneak back in.

WHAT YOU SEE (and what you think you see)	CORE BELIEF	THOUGHTS	FEELINGS	BEHAVIOR
What you see: Young woman walking down street. What you think you see: "That girl is hot and she wants it."	"I'm a weakling." "No one could really love me."	"I'll show her what a man can do." "She wants sex, so she must want sex from me."	Arousal. Feeling wanted. Excitement.	Start rubbing self. Stalk the woman.
What you see: What you think you see:				
What you see: What you think you see:				

Beliefs About "Needs"

There are certain things that we *think* we "need." But a true "need" is something that you must have to survive: like food, water, air, and shelter. Many of the things that you believe you "need" – things that you think you *must* have to get through the day – really aren't needs at all. Let's look at the thoughts you have about the following "needs."

"Need" for sex: ______________________________

____

____

"Need" for love from another person: ______________________________

____

____

"Need" for power or control: ______________________________

____

____

"Need" for excitement: ______________________________

____

____

"Need" to prove your intelligence: ______________________________

____

____

"Need" to let out your anger: ______________________________

____

____

Beliefs About Needs Worksheet

Using your work from the previous page, write down the "needs" that you believed you had to have, which may be connected to your abusive behavior.

Needs Met by Abuse	Beliefs About Needs	Automatic Thoughts Related to Needs and Beliefs
"Need" for sex.		
"Need" for love from another.		
"Need" for power.		
"Need" for excitement.		
"Need" to prove intelligence.		
"Need" to let out your anger.		

Detailed Analysis of My Abusive Behavior Pattern

The purpose of this worksheet is to better understand yourself and your abusive behavior by looking closely at your thoughts, feelings, behaviors, and beliefs at three different times: before you committed the abuse, during the abuse, immediately after the abuse, today, and even in the future. But you need to be honest with yourself if you want to really understand yourself and gain control over your negative feelings and behavior.

Before the Abuse

Feelings: What were you feeling in the hours and minutes before your abuse? Were you turned on, excited, angry, scared? What were you feeling inside?____________________

____

____

"Needs": What "need" was strongest before committing the abuse? Look at your answers to the previous worksheet, "Beliefs About Needs." Why do you think that need was the strongest for you?____

____

____

Thoughts: What do you think about in the time before committing the abuse? Is there a particular thought in your head before you abuse? __________________________

____

____

Behaviors: What actions did you take to put yourself in the position to abuse? What were you doing in the hours prior to the abuse? What actions did you take to trick or manipulate your victim before the abuse? ____________________________________

____

____

Beliefs: Before the abuse, what did you believe about yourself or your values? What did you once believe was true, but now know was wrong? __________________________

____

____

During the Abuse

Feelings: What were you feeling during the abuse? Were you feeling powerful, ashamed, excited, angry, scared? What were you feeling inside? ______________________________

____

____

____

"Needs": What "need" was strongest during the abuse? Was it your belief that you "needed" sex, love from another, power, excitement, to prove yourself, or to let out your anger? Why do you think that need was the strongest during the abuse?_______________

____

____

____

Thoughts: What did you think about when you were committing the abuse? Was there a particular thought in your head as you abused someone? ___________________________

____

____

____

Behaviors: What actions did you take during the abuse? ____________________________

____

____

____

Beliefs: What did you believe about yourself or your values during the abuse? _________

____

____

____

After the Abuse

Feelings: What were you feeling inside on the day after the abuse? Were you feeling powerful, ashamed, excited, angry, scared?____

"Needs": What "need" was strongest on the day after the abuse? Was it your belief that you "needed" sex, love from another, power, excitement, to prove yourself, or to let out your anger? Why do you think that need was the strongest after the abuse?________________

Thoughts: What did you think about after you abused? Was there a particular thought in your head after you abused? ____

Behaviors: What actions did you take after committing the abuse? What things did you do in the hours and the day after the abuse? ____________________________________

Beliefs: What did you believe about yourself or your values in the hours and the day after committing the abuse? ____

Today – When I Think About My Abusive Behavior

Feelings: When you think about your abusive behavior today, what feelings do you have inside? Be honest. ____________________

____

____

____

My beliefs that I know are wrong: Write down some beliefs about yourself or your values that you once thought were true, but now know are wrong. ____________________

____

____

____

My beliefs that others say are wrong: Write down some beliefs about yourself and your values that you believe are right, but others say are wrong. ____________________

____

____

____

My beliefs that are healthy: Write down beliefs about yourself and your values that are healthy. ____________________

____

____

____

Beliefs about what is most important: Write down your beliefs about what is most important to you? ____________________

____

____

____

Beliefs about self: What are your thoughts/beliefs about yourself and what gives you the most self-pride?

Beliefs about sex: What are your thoughts/beliefs about sex and sexuality today?

Beliefs about closeness: What are your thoughts/beliefs about being close to others? How do you feel about trusting others?

Beliefs about purpose: What are your thoughts/beliefs about your purpose in life?

Beliefs about spirituality and meaning: What are your thoughts/beliefs about spirituality, religion, and a higher power?

Looking to the Future

One year from now: Where do you see yourself one year from today? What would you be doing? Where would you like to be?________________________________

____

____

____

____

Getting there: What will you need to learn and what will you need to do in order to get where you would like to be in the future? ____________________________

____

____

____

____

Five years from now: What are your thoughts/beliefs about where you will be and what you will be doing in 5 years? ____________________________________

____

____

____

____

Ten years from now: What are your thoughts/beliefs about what you will be doing in 10 years? ____

____

____

____

____

Pictures of me: Use the space below to draw two pictures of yourself. On the left side, draw a picture of you today. On the right side, draw a picture of yourself in five years.

Me – today	Me – five years from now

Abuse Beliefs Summary Sheet

	BEFORE ABUSE	DURING ABUSE	AFTER ABUSE	NOW	5 YEARS FROM NOW
FEELINGS					
"NEEDS"					
THOUGHTS					
BEHAVIORS					

Abuse Beliefs Summary Sheet (page two)

	BEFORE ABUSE	DURING ABUSE	AFTER ABUSE	NOW	5 YEARS FROM NOW
BELIEFS ABOUT WHAT YOU "NEED"					
BELIEFS ABOUT YOUR SELF AND SELF-PRIDE					
BELIEFS ABOUT SEX AND SEXUAL-ITY					
BELIEFS ABOUT WHAT IS RIGHT AND WRONG. (VALUES & MORALS)					

Abuse Beliefs Summary Sheet (page three)

	BEFORE ABUSE	DURING ABUSE	AFTER ABUSE	NOW	5 YEARS FROM NOW
BELIEFS ABOUT CLOSENESS					
BELIEFS ABOUT YOUR PURPOSE					
BELIEFS ABOUT WHO IS RESPONSIBLE FOR YOUR BEHAVIOR					
BELIEFS ABOUT SPRITUALITY AND HIGHER POWER					

Using Self Talk to Change Negative Beliefs

It is helpful to talk to your therapist and other people about your feelings and thoughts. But you can also talk to *yourself*. Yes, you can actually *talk yourself into feeling better*. This is called "self talk." It takes practice, but if you get good at it, it can help you to handle painful feelings. Here are some examples of using self talk to feel better.

Negative Thought	Positive Self Talk
"I'll never succeed in getting my GED…"	"I've passed in school before. (I'm not in first grade am I?) Therefore, I can get through this too."
"No one likes me…"	"I have had a friend before. One of my best friends was _______________. Therefore, it can't be true that no one likes me."
"I'll never have a girlfriend…"	"I have never asked someone out for a date. I have to start with a date first, and then get to know the person."

Now it's your turn to try. Write down a negative thought in the left column. Write down the type of cognitive distortion in the second column. Then use some positive "self talk" to talk yourself out of the negative thought.

Negative Thought	Type of Cognitive Distortion	Self Talk Positive Response

Positive Self Talk Worksheet

Here are some more examples of positive self talk. Add some negative thoughts of your own and practice changing them with positive self talk.

Negative Thoughts	Positive Self Talk
"I'm out of control and I'm gonna tear this place apart!"	"I'm very angry, yes, but I can control my anger."
"I'm such a stupid loser. Why did I do that?"	"Everyone makes mistakes. I'll do better next time."
"I'll never get over this."	"I'll be OK tomorrow."

Practice Changing "Needs" Into "Wants"

You have learned that "needs" are things that are necessary to survive, like food, air, water, and shelter. Sex is not a need. Power is not a need. If you believe that something you want is a "need," you think that you *must* have it, which leads to anger and frustration. But if you tell yourself that the thing is only something you would like, it is not so frustrating. Practice changing some of your "needs" (things you believe you *must* have) into "wants" (things you would *like* to have). This is a realistic alternative that can be achieved with effort.

"NEEDS" (irrational) "I used to believe that I needed…"	"WANTS" (rational) "But what I really would like is…"
I used to believe that: I "need" power and control.	But what I really would like is: To balance my desire for power over others with closeness and trust and to balance my desire for control with flexibility and spontaneity.
I used to believe that: I "need" excitement.	But what I really would like is to:
I used to believe that: I "need" love from another.	But what I really would like is to:
I used to believe that: I "need" to prove myself.	But what I really would like is to:
I used to believe that: I "need" to vent my anger.	But what I really would like is to:
I used to believe that: I "need" sex.	But what I really would like is to:

Negative Beliefs Come From Your Experiences

Negative beliefs and thoughts lead to negative feelings, which then lead to negative behaviors. When you learn to change the negative belief, it is in your power to change the negative feelings and the behavior.

For example, if you *thought* that a man stepped on your foot on purpose, you might *feel* angry and *behave* by giving him a shove.

But, if you *thought* it was an accident, you might only *feel* annoyed and would *behave* by giving more space to the person.

And if you turn and find that the man is blind, your *thought* would be it was an accident and you would probably *feel* pity and might *behave* by helping him find his way.

Thus your feelings and behavior will be different depending on your thoughts about the negative event of having someone step on your foot.

You're probably wondering where did all this negative thinking come from? Why do I have so many negative thoughts? Why do I have so many negative beliefs?

It all comes from experience. If you grew up around people that were kind and supportive, you would tend to have more positive thoughts about yourself and other people. But if you grew up with lots of criticism, or physical or sexual abuse, you tend to have a lot of negative thoughts.

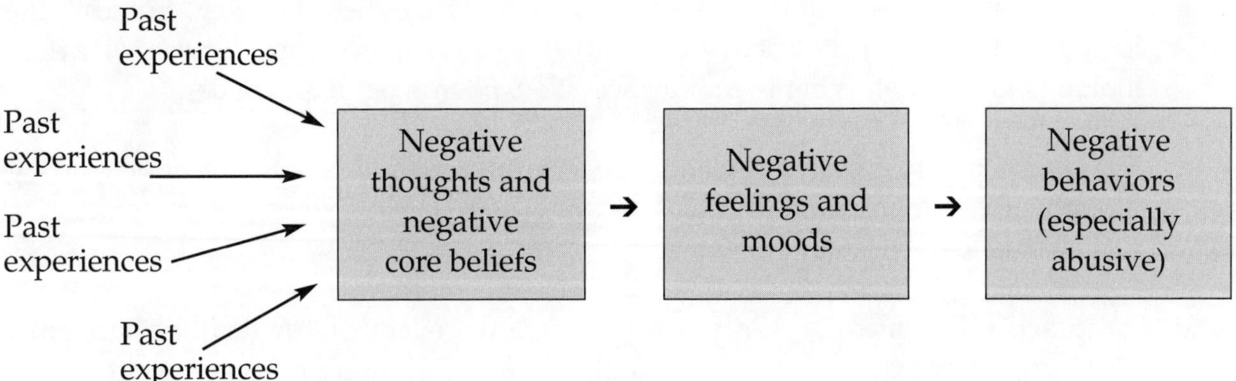

The sad part is that you can't change the past. You can't go back in time and give yourself perfect parents and a perfect home. But the good part is that you *can* change the negative thinking and negative beliefs that you learned growing up. Negative thinking is like any bad habit. Trying to quit smoking is really hard, but it is a habit that can be changed. Negative thoughts can be changed too. It takes a lot of practice, but you can learn to think positive. And positive thinking will change your attitude about yourself, your life, your views about sex, and your view of the world.

How to Change Negative Thinking When It Happens

Your goal is to be able to recognize negative thinking as soon as it happens so that you can stop it – before it starts causing bad feelings and bad behavior.

Let's look at the steps you can use to stop negative thinking.

Step one Stop	Step two Recognize	Step three Positive self-talk	Step four Check it out

1. The first step is to STOP. When you are in a situation and something negative happens, you need to "stop" before you react. Automatic thoughts can pop into your head so quickly that you react instantly – before you have had time to think about the event. So you need to interrupt your automatic reaction by stopping. You can even say the word "stop" to yourself.

2. If you can interrupt your "automatic" reaction, you have a chance to RECOGNIZE your own negative thinking. You can take a moment to examine your own thinking. You can ask yourself, "What am I thinking right now?" "What do I think about what just happened?"

3. The third step is POSITIVE SELF-TALK. Ask yourself if your thought or belief is accurate or true. Ask yourself if it may be a cognitive distortion. Try to "test" the idea. Is it all true, partly true, a little bit true, or unknown? Consider other ways of looking at the event. What is another way to explain what happened?

4. The last step is to CHECK IT OUT. Compare the two ideas: the negative starting thought, and the positive self-talk thought. Which belief is stronger? Which one do you choose to believe?

Now let's practice this method. Write down a negative event or trigger that happened today. Then write down the negative thought that you had about that trigger event.

Negative trigger event: ______________________________

Negative thought about event: ______________________________

____

____

STOP and RECOGNIZE. Before the negative thought creates negative feelings and behavior, stop a moment. Tell yourself that this may be "stinkin' thinkin'. Take time to recognize that the negative thought is probably a cognitive distortion. Remember that negative thinking is not reality. The negative thought is just your perception or opinion about reality, but the thought itself is not reality.

Now SELF TALK. Tell yourself that there is another way to look at the same negative event. Come up with a different way to explain what happened. Write down a more positive belief about the negative trigger event. ____

____

____

____

Now CHECK OUT the new thought. Which belief is stronger? The first one, or the second one? Why? ____

____

____

____

Now that you have recognized the thought as a cognitive distortion, rate how much you believe in the first and the second thoughts:

	Rate belief from 0 to 10
The original negative thought?	______________
The positive alternative?	______________

What if it didn't work?

What do you do if you find that you still believe the original negative thought more than you believe the positive thought? Don't worry. It's okay. Negative thinking and negative beliefs are tough to change.

If you find that you still believe *more* in the negative thought, go to the next page and do the following:

What to do when you're stuck...

What do you *feel* when you believe the first negative thought? When you think the negative thought, what emotion(s) are you feeling and how strong is it? ______________________

____

____

____

____

Now imagine what you *might feel* if you had a stronger belief in the positive thought? How would you feel inside if you really believed the positive thought? ______________________

____

____

____

____

Which feeling is better? If you could choose one feeling over the other, which one would you pick? Why? ____

____

____

____

____

Changing Cognitive Distortions of Abusive Behavior and Violence

Write down some of your cognitive distortions related to abuse and aggression. Then use positive self talk to come up with alternative positive ideas.

Cognitive Distortion (irrational)	Positive Self Talk (rational)
Example: "I wouldn't have hit him if he just cooperated with me."	"I have self control. It was my choice to hit him. I wanted to feel powerful.
Example: "If he's wearing a leather coat that cool, he better be tough enough to keep it."	

CHAPTER 7
RESPONSIBILITY

From Denial to Responsibility

In this chapter, you will learn about the many ways that abusers deny their behaviors and try to escape responsibility for the harm they have caused to victims. There are many different kinds of "denial." It can range from total denial of having done anything wrong ("lying") to denying any need for treatment. Over the course of treatment, most abusers go through various stages of denial – and hopefully, they begin taking more and more responsibility for their actions.

The diagram below shows the different stages of denial, starting at the lowest level ("lying") and building to the highest level ("taking full responsibility").

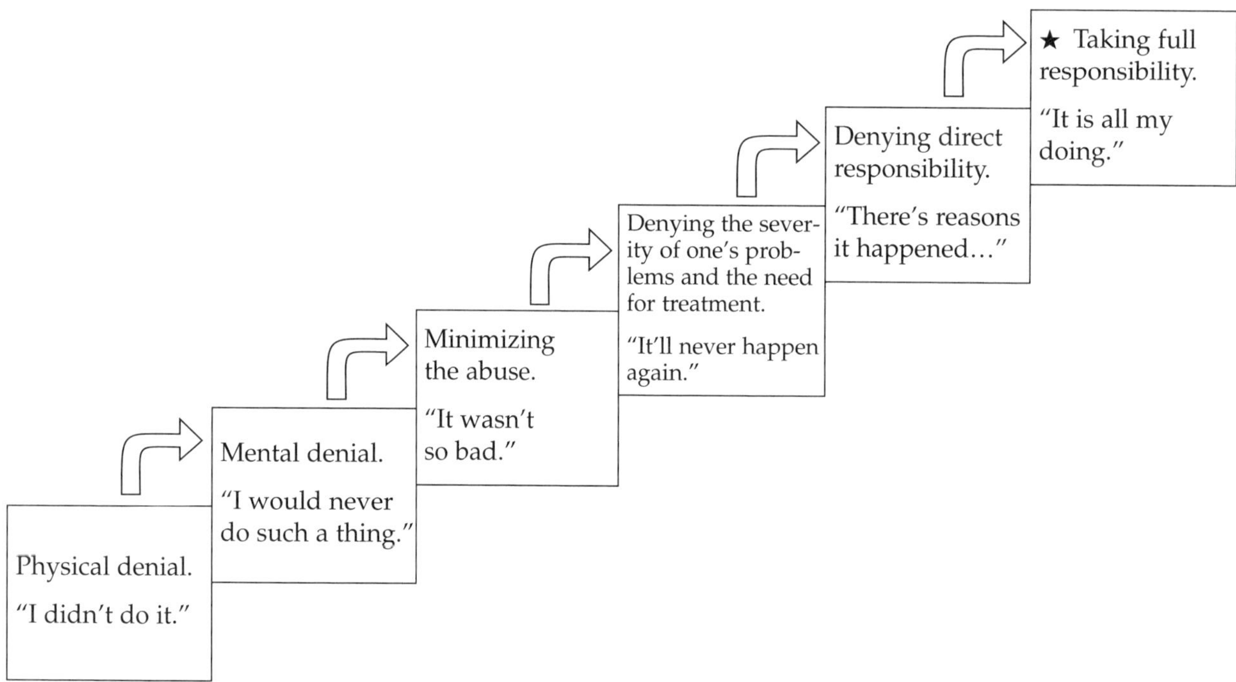

1. Physical denial – lying to everyone.

Physical denial means denying the specific abuse ever happened. Even when the evidence is overwhelming, some abusers will "lie and deny" that they committed any abuse at all. Some abusers will make up a false alibi for the day of the crime. Sometimes, abusers will even get family or friends to join their lie and support the false alibi. Here are three examples of physical denial:

- Tony's mother and stepfather both insisted that he was with them at a ball game in a neighboring town at the time of the abuse. The parents claimed that he was seen by many observers. When Tony's attorney asked them to produce even one witness who could substantiate the alibi, they did not and claimed that "his friends are too busy." When pressed for the names of witnesses, the parents refused to give them. Even after Tony was found guilty by the court, his parents continued to claim his innocence and blamed the conviction on the attorney's incompetence. Tony later refused to participate in treatment.

- Paul was arrested for dragging a young woman into the bushes with a knife at her throat and robbing her before she was able to escape. The woman knew Paul and identified him to the police. One of Paul's friends also witnessed the attack and supported the victim's story to the police. Nonetheless, Paul's parents claimed he was with them at the time of the assault.

Physical denial can be the toughest to treat because abusers such as Tony and Paul do not accept any responsibility for their behavior. They claim it never happened or they had no part in it. Since they denied their behavior, they also will not admit to planning the act or having fantasies before the act. When confronted with the facts, they show no guilt or shame. Instead, they may show outrage and righteous indignation. "How can you accuse me of this!" "I would never do that!" Some abusers will claim to be the victim of false allegations or will claim that the victim or the system is out to get them. They show no regret or remorse, nor pity for the victim. And, since they claim that they did nothing wrong, they will not admit to any need to change their abusive behavior. When family members support physical denial, it is even more difficult to get the abuser to participate in treatment.

2. Mental denial – lying to self.

Some abusers will deny the overall charge by avoiding the particular details of the behavior. Rather than saying, "I couldn't have done it because I wasn't there at the time," they will claim, "I'm not the kind of person who would do that." They avoid the details of the behavior. They don't care if it happened on June 6th or June 7th. While their families may sometimes join the abuser's denial, it is not as bad as when the family actually lies to protect the abuser with a false alibi. Chances of treatment are better with these families because they often will support treatment once they are convinced that the abuser is guilty.

Like physical denial, abusers who are mental deniers also deny any reason to change their abusive behavior because they deny it. Since they claim innocence, they also deny any plans or fantasies prior to the act. And, since they claim that they did nothing wrong, they will not admit to any need to change their behavior. Mental deniers also show no regret or remorse, nor pity for the victim. And they often pretend to be outraged at the accusations.

3. Minimizing the abuse.

Many abusers will admit parts of their behavior, but deny the rest. This frequently happens with abusers who have many victims, but are caught with just one victim. Such abusers may agree to get treatment, but they withhold information about other victims and the number of the acts because they want to avoid additional charges with the same victim or other undisclosed victims or acts. Sometimes they will admit to a less serious act to avoid harsher punishment, such as admitting to fondling a child, but denying penetration.

In most cases, abusers will deny the extent of the behavior or their problems. Shame and embarrassment leads them to hide how often, how long and how many acts they have really committed. The abuser's story often contradicts the story told by the victim.

Abusers will also minimize the extent of their behavior by denying that they planned the abuse or had fantasies prior to the behavior – even when the facts show obvious planning was needed to prevent discovery.

Abusers will also deny the extent of their behavior by refusing to admit that they planned the act or had fantasies prior to the behavior – even when the facts show obvious planning was needed to prevent discovery.

In addition, they typically minimize the extent of harm they have caused their victims. When asked directly, they may proclaim loudly that they did commit the behavior, but they are unable to specify in what way the behavior was harmful. They rarely admit planning. While they are often distraught and remorseful after discovery, there is often no real sense of internalized guilt. They underestimate the difficulty of change, and feel that simply deciding not to abuse again will be sufficient to stop it from happening again.

4. Denying the severity of the problem and the need for treatment.

Even when abusers admit the full extent of their behavior, they often minimize the severity of their problems. Many tell themselves that their behavior "was no big deal" or "not so bad after all." They want to believe that their victims have recovered from the abuse without any lasting harm. This denial protects the abuser from the guilt and shame he would feel if he admitted the damage he has caused.

When abusers continue to under-estimate the impact of their behavior, they remain at serious risk of doing it again. It is a short step from thinking, "I didn't do any real harm," to thinking that, "one more time won't really matter." By denying the severity of his problems, the abuser can tell himself/herself that he really doesn't need treatment. He may deny the need for treatment by saying, "That's all in the past," or "The best thing for me is not to think about it," or "I know what I did and talking about it won't change anything." The problem just doesn't go away by itself. If an abuser does not deal with his problem and learn better ways of handling negative anti-social urges, he will not know what to do when he finds himself in future situations that arouse those urges. He remains the same person he was when abusive. He has the same urges and has no skills to control those urges.

It takes a lot of courage for an abuser to face how much damage has been caused to the victim(s) and how much damage can never be repaired. It takes courage to go into treatment and make a commitment to change.

Some abusers use religion as a way to avoid treatment and responsibility. They will claim that they have been "saved" or "seen the light" and will trust in God alone for strength. In other words, everything is magically fixed and they will not have to do the hard work of facing their problems and learning how to control them. As much as they want to believe it, religious salvation alone is simply not enough. Religion can be a great comfort and aid to abusers, but only if the abuser takes the attitude that, "God helps those who help themselves." The abuser proves his sincerity by asking God for support as he works hard in treatment to change his behavior. The abuser will not expect God to do the work of treatment for him, but uses his faith to keep doing the work. The abuser should see God and religion as helpful to him in changing his behavior through treatment – not that God eliminates the need for treatment.

5. Denial of responsibility – through blame.

Some abusers may admit to the behavior, agree that it is wrong, and acknowledge that the problem is serious, but they do not take responsibility for the behavior. In the final type of denial, the abuser will blame his unacceptable behavior on some other reason. The most common excuse is "I was drunk" or "I was high at the time." The abuser insists that he would never have done what he did without being drunk or high. Therefore, it was not really his fault and the problem is cured if he stops drinking or using.

Abusers will give "reasons" to explain why they abuse. They will explain all the things that caused them to do it. Abusers will blame their behavior on other people or situations, such as problems at work, or nagging wives, or poverty, or loneliness, or a bad neighborhood: "Yes it happened, but there were a lot of reasons for it…" Instead of taking responsibility, the abuser makes it look like *he* was the real victim. He will complain that he lost his family, his freedom, his job, and his respect in the community – as if it is worse than the harm he committed against his victims. He feels worse about the damage he has suffered himself rather than the damage he caused to others.

Admitting to anti-social urges and planning is extremely important for this type of denial. Abusers cannot achieve genuine acceptance of responsibility without it. To admit to anti-social fantasies is to admit arousal and pleasure in the abuse. To admit to planning the abuse is to admit how much effort went into setting up the victim and preventing discovery.

6. Taking full responsibility.

When an abuser achieves full responsibility, his story of the extent of his abuse will match that of his victim. He understands he cannot "undo" the abuse and appreciates the severe damage caused to his victim. He feels guilt for his behavior and the harm it has caused. He admits how much his abusive behavior was preceded by fantasies, the extent to which he planned the abuse, and the ways he manipulated and controlled his victims. He does not believe that change will be easy, and he recognizes an ongoing temptation to re-abuse. He admits to fears of his behavior again and maintains a healthy fear of losing control over his abusive behavior.

Types of Denial

Abusers deny their problems and their abuses in so many ways. Look through the following list of different types of denial. Which ones have you used? Be honest. Put a checkmark "√" next to the types of denial that you have used.

	Deny the facts of the abuse.
	Deny awareness of having committed an abuse or of having caused harm.
	Deny that the abuse has caused serious harm.
	Deny responsibility for the abuse.
	Deny manipulating the victim to make it easier to abuse.
	Deny getting turned on by inappropriate sexual interests.
	Deny any wrong behavior at all.
	Deny some abuses, while admitting to other abuses.
	Deny by minimizing the severity of the abusive behavior.
	Deny hurting the victim.
	Deny by rationalizing.
	Deny other deviant behaviors.
	Deny planning the abuse, e.g., "It just happened." "I just happened to be in the park."
	Deny denial: "I'm telling you the honest truth!"
	Deny having a problem now, e.g., "Now that I know it's wrong, it won't happen again." "It's all in my past. I'm cured." "It was a one time thing."
	Deny the difficulty to change, e.g., "All I need to do is stay away from drugs."
	Deny the risk of relapse, e.g., "I've got it all under control."
	Deny through silence, e.g., "If they don't know, why tell them."
	Deny the seriousness of effects.

Go back through the list. Of all the items that you marked, which type of denial do you use the most? Circle it. What do you gain from that kind of denial? ____________________

____

____

Denial Worksheet

List five types of denial that you have used in your behavior and give a real-life example of each:

1. ______________________________

____

2. ______________________________

____

3. ______________________________

____

4. ______________________________

____

5. ______________________________

____

What did you gain from using denial about your behavior? For example, did you escape punishment? Did you avoid feeling bad about yourself? Did you give yourself permission to abuse again? What did you gain? ______________________________

____

____

____

____

____

Describe some thoughts and self talk that you used to deny when you were abusive?

1. ____
____

2. ____
____

3. ____
____

4. ____
____

5. ____
____

Describe the ways you used denial so you wouldn't have to feel bad about the harm that you caused to your victim and the victim's family. ____

____
____
____
____
____
____
____
____

Taking Responsibility Exercise

When you are confronted with your behavior, do you try to gain sympathy by making it look like you were the victim? When you are confronted with your behavior, do you still say, "Yes I did, but..." Do you blame other people or your situation for your abusive behavior? Do you say that is your teachers' fault, your parents' fault, your therapist's fault, your victim's fault, or society's fault? Do you say, "I couldn't help it? I was just getting what I needed." If you answer yes, you are not taking responsibility.

To succeed in treatment, you will need to take full responsibility for everything that you have done to hurt others. You will need to take full responsibility for your acting out, your aggression, your lying, and your trickery and manipulation of others.

Taking responsibility is a very difficult thing for abusers to do. Taking responsibility is also an important key to success in treatment. When an abuser takes full responsibility for his abusive behavior, he must do so without any "buts..." One of the most common "buts" is when the abuser claims that he was himself a victim of abuse – and that is why he acts like he does.

Even if you were also the victim of sexual, physical, or emotional abuse, it can never be used as an excuse for your own abuses. No matter what horrible things may have happened to you, it never gives you the right to victimize someone else. If you were hurt, your responsibility is to address your own damage in treatment so that you can gain control of your behavior and never abuse any more victims. You are responsible for changing your behavior and you cannot avoid responsibility by falling into self-pity or giving yourself "good" reasons for acting badly.

Let's start with the responsibility exercise on the following page. Think about one of your abuses. On the left side, write down the thoughts that you had before or during the abuse. These are the negative thoughts you used to avoid responsibility or to put the responsibility on your victim or the situation. Be honest with yourself and rate how strongly you believe each thought from 1 (not at all) to 10 (very much).

Then try to change that thought into a new idea that takes full responsibility for what happened. What is wrong with the belief or thought on the left? Write down a rational positive belief on the right side that shows that you are taking full responsibility.

PUTTING RESPONSIBILITY ON THE VICTIM FOR MY ACTIONS	RATE BELIEF	TAKING RESPONSIBILITY FOR MY OWN ACTIONS	RATE BELIEF
Example: It was his fault for disrespecting me.	1	I disrespected him too. And I could have walked away from a fight.	9
Example: If she didn't want sex, she could have just stopped me.	2	I had all the power and control over a weaker person so she did what I wanted.	8

Start a new chart and again make a list of thoughts and rate the percent of responsibility. If you are honest, each time you repeat this exercise, you will be taking more and more responsibility.

How Abusers Avoid Responsibility

Abusers try to escape responsibility for their behavior. There are a number of cognitive distortions and tricks they use to deceive others and escape responsibility. Put a checkmark "√" next to ones that you have used.

	Silence: The abuser uses silence to maintain secrecy. He does not talk, or respond or participate. He says things like, "I don't know", "I don't care", "No comment", "I forgot", and "I can't explain why."
	Just tell 'em what they want to hear: The abuser figures out what he thinks the other person wants to hear and then says it. "If he wants me to show remorse, I'll pretend to feel remorse." "He wants me to say my belief is a cognitive distortion, so I'll tell him it's a cognitive distortion."
	Lying: The abuser never tells the truth. He lies by making things up. He lies by leaving things out. He lies by pretending to agree.
	Confusing: The abuser says things that are unclear, vague, unrelated or confusing to distract the listener and avoid dealing with his problem. He does not stay focused on the issue.
	Minimizing: The abuser tries to make his abusive behavior look less serious, small, or not important. "It only happened once." "The insurance will pay for a new car."
	Switching: The abuser changes the subject to avoid dealing with his problem. "When you mentioned my abuse, it reminded me of when my father used to beat me.
	Pretending to agree: The abuser pretends to agree so that the other person will stop confronting him with the problem. "I see what you mean." "Yes, I need to take more responsibility." "Yes, I should definitely do that…"
	Only hears what he wants to hear: The abuser ignores criticism or information that does not support his beliefs or that makes him look bad. He only pays attention to information that makes him look good or gives him a good excuse for acting badly. For example, the abuser says, "I'm the best in group because you said I "say more in group than anybody else." But he ignored the more important comment that he was "too busy talking to listen to anybody else."
	"You don't understand me!": The abuser accuses others of misunderstanding him. Therefore he refuses to say anything more. "I tried to tell you, but you don't understand, so forget it!" He tries to make it look like he's making an effort and it is their fault if they don't understand.
	Better than the others: This is the abuser who tries to look good by making others look worse or by comparing his crimes to worse crimes. He will say, "I just broke into the houses, I didn't mug anybody," or "I only looked in windows, I didn't hurt anybody." He draws attention to the mistakes and failings of others to escape attention to his own problems. "I'm the only one who does his homework." "They broke the rules, not me."
	Bad memory: The abuser does not remember information he wants to keep secret or pretends that he doesn't remember or pretends that he did not understand. "I can't be expected to remember every little detail." "That was ten years ago, I don't remember." "I didn't understand what you meant."
	I'm cured: The abuser thinks that he has already solved his problems without making any real change. "I quit drinking, so it can never happen again." "I finished the class, now let me out of here."
	Black-and-white thinking: The abuser can only see things one way and that's his way. He will not consider another opinion. He will not try to see things from the other person's view. He cannot see the middle ground in any idea or conflict. "She wasn't wearing a bra, so of course she wanted sex." "A man has to be tough."
	The best defense is a good offense: The abuser attacks others to take the attention off himself/herself. He uses anger and arguments to intimidate others and get them to stop confronting him. "This program stinks…" "You lied." "Look what *you* did…" or "You don't have the proper training."

** Adapted from Yolchelson & Samenow*

Go back through the list of ways that abusers avoid responsibility and avoid changing themselves. How many did you mark? Which ones do you use most often? Choose the trick that you use most often. Name it and then describe how and when you use this trick to avoid responsibility. ____

____

____

____

____

____

Responsibility and Self-Management Skills

Intensive Treatment Phase

Level Three
Incorporation

Congratulations for reaching the Incorporation level of the workbook. "Incorporation" means putting everything together. Now you can begin to incorporate the knowledge and skills you learned in the Gaining Knowledge and Application levels of the treatment program into your daily thinking, behavior and lifestyle. You will be pulling everything together to reach a higher level in managing negative thinking and negative core beliefs, while also building a better self-image and sense of responsibility.

The Incorporation level begins with the Healthy Behavior chapter, which will help you strengthen your ability to look at negative events and situations in a new, positive way. The goal is to free yourself from the negative thoughts and beliefs that have held you back for so long and to gain a better understanding and appreciation of life and its challenges.

As you move through this level of the Workbook and the treatment program, you will be focusing on many of the following key areas:

Chapter 8. Healthy Behavior	• Increasing awareness of your experience of anger and hurt feelings so you can learn better self-control of strong emotions. • Learning how to think in healthy, realistic ways that support a more consistent positive attitude and sense of self-control. • Learning how to stop unwanted thoughts and urges. • Learning how to use positive thinking to beat bad moods and defeat negative beliefs.
Chapter 9. Substance Abuse and Acting Out	• Learning about the negative impact of drug and alcohol use on your thinking and acting out behavior.
Chapter 10. Empathy	• Developing a sincere concern for the pain and damage experienced by victims of crime and violence. • Learning about the many and long-lasting harmful effects of abuse and violence on victims, both adults and children.
Chapter 11. Victim to Victimizer to Survivor	• Looking at how your own victimization is connected to the negative beliefs, thoughts, feelings and behavior that play a part in your inappropriate behavior. • Learning to understand the impact of your own victimization without *ever* using it to excuse, minimize or justify *any* acts of violence, abuse or offending.
Chapter 12. Mental Health and Medication Management	• Learning about your own mental health, how to manage mental illness, and, if applicable, how medication helps to control mental illness.

Chapter 8
Healthy Behavior

Worksheet: How Do I Experience and Express Anger?

People feel anger in different ways. The goal of this exercise is to see how you feel and show anger. Many people do not really know how their anger feels. Some do not even know when they are feeling angry. Others have trouble seeing the difference between fear or anger or frustration.

Begin by thinking about something that makes you feel angry. Then, close your eyes and try to feel inside your body. Take a trip through the different parts of your body – your feet, legs, arms, shoulders, hips, guts, chest, neck, face – and see how it feels in that particular spot.

Then go through the following check-list to describe how anger feels in your own body. Put a check mark "√" beside the things that you do when you are angry. If you have physical feelings in some part of your body that are not on the list, go ahead and add the feeling to the list.

____ 1. Muscle tension (where?)____

____ 2. Change in breathing (how?)____

____ 3. Sick feeling (where?) ____

____ 4. Tight feeling (where?) ____

____ 5. Change in posture (how?) ____

____ 6. Empty feeling (where?)____

____ 7. Face changes color (how?) ____

____ 8. Change in temperature (how?) ____

____ 9. Change in energy level (how?) ____

____10. Change in heart rate (how?)____

____11. Throbbing (where?)____

____12. Change in voice (how?) ____

____13. Other (describe) ____

____14. Other (describe) ____

____15. Other (describe) ____

People act differently when they are angry. Go through the following list and put a check mark "√" beside the things that you do when you are angry.

____ 1. I yell or scream.
____ 2. I cry.
____ 3. I go off to be alone.
____ 4. I hit a person.
____ 5. I hit things.
____ 6. I pace the room.
____ 7. I read.
____ 8. I drink alcohol.
____ 9. I hit or hurt myself.
____ 10. I get high on drugs.
____ 11. I can't stop thinking about it.
____ 12. I break something.
____ 13. I run away.
____ 14. I eat and eat.
____ 15. I just hold it in.
____ 16. I think about suicide.
____ 17. I get angry.
____ 18. I go beat someone up.
____ 19. I keep calm and talk out my feelings.
____ 20. I complain about it.
____ 21. I write out my feelings.
____ 22. I give the silent treatment.
____ 23. I curse and swear.
____ 24. I say something sarcastic.
____ 25. I do something creative.
____ 26. I punch the wall.
____ 27. I do exercise like running or sports.
____ 28. I make a list of things to do.
____ 29. I say something nasty.
____ 30. I say something to hurt the person back.
____ 31. I take my anger out on someone else (not the other person involved).
____ 32. I take revenge.
____ 33. I masturbate or find sex.
____ 34. I sleep.
____ 35. I talk to a friend or supportive person.
____ 36. I sexually abuse someone.
____ 37. I watch TV.
____ 38. I talk out my feelings a little later.
____ 39. I change my thinking about the situation.
____ 40. Other things I do: ____________________

Put an "X" beside the negative and destructive ways that you express your anger. What happens after you do show your anger in these negative ways? Do you ever get a good outcome from a negative action? ____

____

____

____

Now, go through the list and circle all of the positive and healthy ways that you could use to express anger. How many do you use now? What would be different for yourself and others if you used some of these positive ways of expressing anger? Why?

____

____

____

What kind of situation triggers your anger? ____________________________________

____

____

____

____

What do you usually tell yourself (think) in these situations? ____________________

____

____

____

____

What could you tell yourself (think) to help you feel less anger? _________________

____

____

____

____

Charlene Steen, Relapse Prevention Workbook for Youth in Treatment, 1993.

Worksheet: How Do I Experience and Express Hurt Feelings?

People experience hurt feelings in different ways. The goal of this exercise is to see how you experience and express hurt feelings. Many people do not really know how they respond when they feel hurt.

Begin by thinking about something that has hurt your feelings. Then, close your eyes and try to feel inside your body. Take a trip through the different parts of your body – your feet, legs, arms, shoulders, hips, guts, chest, neck, face – and see how it feels in that particular spot.

Then go through the following check-list to describe what it is like inside your body when your feelings are hurt. Put a check mark "√" beside the things that you do when your feelings are hurt. If you have physical feelings in some part of your body that are not on the list, go ahead and add the feeling to the list.

____ 1. Muscle tension (where?) ____________________

____ 2. Change in breathing (how?) ____________________

____ 3. Sick feeling (where?) ____________________

____ 4. Tight feeling (where?) ____________________

____ 5. Change in posture (how?) ____________________

____ 6. Empty feeling (where?) ____________________

____ 7. Face changes color (how?) ____________________

____ 8. Change in temperature (how?) ____________________

____ 9. Change in energy level (how?) ____________________

____ 10. Change in heart rate (how?) ____________________

____ 11. Throbbing (where?) ____________________

____ 12. Change in voice (how?) ____________________

____ 13. Other (describe) ____________________

____ 14. Other (describe) ____________________

____ 15. Other (describe) ____________________

People act differently when their feelings are hurt. Go through the following list and put a check mark "√" beside the things that you do when your feelings are hurt.

____ 1. I yell or scream.

____ 2. I cry.

____ 3. I go off to be alone.

____ 4. I hit a person.

____ 5. I hit things.

____ 6. I pace the room.

____ 7. I read.

____ 8. I drink alcohol.

____ 9. I hit or hurt myself.

____ 10. I get high on drugs.

____ 11. I can't stop thinking about it.

____ 12. I break something.

____ 13. I run away.

____ 14. I eat and eat.

____ 15. I just hold it in.

____ 16. I think about suicide.

____ 17. I get angry.

____ 18. I go beat someone up.

____ 19. I keep calm and talk out my feelings.

____ 20. I complain about it.

____ 21. I write out my feelings.

____ 21. I write out my feelings.

____ 22. I give the silent treatment.

____ 23. I curse and swear.

____ 24. I say something sarcastic.

____ 25. I do something creative.

____ 26. I punch the wall.

____ 27. I do exercise like running, sports.

____ 28. I make a list of things to do.

____ 29. I say something nasty.

____ 30. I say something to hurt the person back.

____ 31. I take my anger out on someone else (not the other person involved).

____ 32. I take revenge.

____ 33. I masturbate or find sex.

____ 34. I sleep.

____ 35. I talk to a friend or supportive person.

____ 36. I sexually abuse someone.

____ 37. I watch TV.

____ 38. I talk out my feelings a little later.

____ 39. I change my thinking about the situation.

____ 40. Other things I do: ______________

____

____

Put an "X" beside the negative and destructive ways that you handle your hurt feelings. What happens after you do show your hurt feelings in these negative ways? Do you ever get a good outcome from one of these negative actions?______________________________

____

____

____

Now, go through the list and circle all of the positive and healthy ways that you could handle your hurt feelings. How many do you use? What would be different for yourself and others if you used some of these positive ways of expressing hurt feelings? Why?________

____

____

____

____

What kind of situations trigger feeling hurt?____________________________

____

____

____

____

What do you usually tell yourself (think) in these situations? ________________

____

____

____

____

What could you tell yourself (think) to help you feel less hurt? ______________

____

____

____

____

How to Stop Unwanted Thoughts and Urges

Many people have sudden urges or thoughts that are inappropriate. These inappropriate thoughts, fantasies and urges can "pop" into one's mind and then trigger more problem thinking and behavior. This can be discouraging to a person who is seriously trying to change his behavior. For example, a person may have urges to beat people up. He knows this is inappropriate and he wants to change, but he does not know how to stop the thoughts.

"Thought stopping" is a method that can help you to stop inappropriate urges and thoughts. Like any skill, this method takes repeated practice. The more you do it, the better it works. Here are the steps of "thought stopping."

		1		2		3		4
Inappropriate or problematic urge or thought	➔	STOP! Yell "stop" to yourself.	➔	SWITCH to good picture	➔	STOP AND THINK about punishment.	➔	GET INTO HEALTHY ACTIVITY

Step 1: Thought stopping. When you have a inappropriate or problematic urge or thought, you should yell "stop" to yourself. Obviously, in most situations you cannot yell out loud. But you can yell in your own head. Yell as loud as you can inside your mind – "STOP!" or "NO!" If you have some privacy, you can say "stop" out loud to yourself.

Step 2: Switch to a good image. After yelling "stop," switch to a mental image of a good, kind person who is important in your life. This could be a friend, sibling, teacher, parent, grandparent, and/or neighbor. This can be anyone who has been good and kind to you, who respects you or cares about you, and that you want to make proud of you. The good image can NEVER be a victim.

Step 3: Stop and think about the negative consequences. Now stop and think about the horrible negative things that can happen if you act on an urge. Pick out the worst consequences that happened to you after people found out about your abuse. What events were the most awful, shameful and painful for you? Some examples are: getting arrested; getting convicted in court; being locked in a youth detention center; telling your family what you did; losing love and respect; losing loved ones; having people look at you with disgust; rumors at school; or seeing the damage you have caused to the victim, his/her family, and your own family. Pick the images that are most painful for you.

Step 4: Get into healthy activity. Probably the most important step is to get busy with something healthy. Don't just sit there. Get up and do something positive. Wash your face with cool water. Go take a walk. Call a friend. Go wash the dishes. Go play with your pet. Pick up your musical instrument. Get out of the room. Do some push-ups or sit-ups. Do whatever you can that is positive and puts your mind on other things other than sex or self-pity.

		1		2		3		4
Problematic urge or thought.	→	STOP! Yell "stop" to yourself.	→	SWITCH to good picture.	→	STOP AND THINK about punishment.	→	GET INTO HEALTHY ACTIVITY

Example:

abuse fantasy	→	"Stop it!"	→	Grandma always cared about me and I always wanted to make her proud of me.	→	It'll ruin my life! The police come to the front door to arrest me and Grandma looks horrified.	→	Healthy activity. Step outside for a breath of fresh air.

Now try it yourself. Fill the blanks with a thought stopping method that can work for you.

URGE	→	STOP!	→	SWITCH	→	STOP AND THINK	→	GET INTO HEALTHY ACTIVITY

Healthy Thinking Leads to Healthy Living

Healthy behavior goes along with healthy thoughts, healthy beliefs and good feelings. You have already learned how negative thoughts and beliefs can create negative feelings and behavior, and how positive thoughts can create positive feelings and behavior.

Look at these two styles of dating behavior. The first person starts with positive, healthy thinking. The second person starts with negative, distorted thinking. See how negative and positive thinking can produce very different feelings and behavior – and outcomes.

Healthy Style (Positive Thinking)								
Thoughts It would be nice to meet her. I wonder what kind of person she is.	→	Feelings Pleasant, excited, happy, a little bit nervous about approaching her.	→	Behavior Talk. Ask to spend some time together.	→	Outcome Good date that could lead to a lasting friendship.	→	New healthy beliefs I'm an interesting and likeable person.
Unhealthy Style (Negative Thinking)								
Thoughts She is so hot. She'd never look at a pervert like me.	→	Feelings Frustrated, scared, lonely, hopeless, angry.	→	Behavior Sit and stare at her until she leaves.	→	Outcome Alone. No date. No friendship.	→	Same old rotten beliefs I'm a loser. She's stuck up.

You can be like the first person who enjoys a healthy life style. The key is healthy thinking. You, too, have the ability to think positive healthy thoughts, which can build positive feelings, positive behavior, and positive outcomes.

When you can identify negative thoughts, you can begin to put them to the test. Is it really true? Or is it just your opinion? Are there any facts to support the idea? Any facts that reject the idea? When you start to challenge negative thoughts and beliefs, you begin to see that most of them are errors. They are cognitive distortions. When you reject negative thinking, things start to change for the better. You can create different thoughts, feelings and behavior – positive ones. You can take positive control of your life.

Let's practice some healthy thinking. Begin by sitting back and closing your eyes. Imagine how you would like to feel. Imagine that today is a great day where you are feeling good and you are proud of yourself. Stay with the good feelings for a few minutes, then come back to this exercise.

Okay. Now write down three or four of the thoughts that you just had while you were feeling good and healthy. Write the healthy thoughts on the left side.

Healthy Thoughts I Had	Healthy Feelings I Had

Now look over the healthy thoughts you just had. No one told you what to think. You did it yourself, naturally. By choosing to imagine a healthy, positive life, you began to create a positive life for yourself. You can choose to think positive thoughts. Now read your healthy thoughts one more time. Close your eyes after reading each one and then feel inside yourself. What feelings did you feel when you imagined healthy thoughts. Use the right side of the chart to describe how you felt inside beside each healthy thought on the left side.

Now let's take it one step further. Take your healthy thought and your good feelings and close your eyes one more time. Imagine how you will act. Imagine what you can do differently because you are thinking and feeling healthy. Write down your new behavior. Do you look different? Stand different? Talk different? Walk different? Act different? Describe how you act differently when you have healthy thoughts. ______________________________

____

____

____

____

____

____

If you met a person who was behaving in the ways you described above, what would you think about that person? Is it someone you would like? Is it a person you would want for a friend? Is it a person you would respect? Is it a person you would trust? Describe your opinion below. ______________________________

____

____

____

____

____

____

Using Positive Thinking to Get Rid of a Bad Mood

Many people think that a "bad mood" is something that you just have to bear. They believe that you wake up in a bad mood and it will last until the day is done. The fact is that bad moods come from negative thinking. You have the power to change a bad mood by using positive thinking. The problem for you and others is that rotten moods and rotten feelings often lead to problem behavior. So it is important for you to learn how to control bad moods and painful emotions, such as loneliness, depression, anger, shyness, guilt, frustration, worry and fear.

This method puts the skills that you have already learned into a step-by-step procedure for changing rotten moods and feelings.

Steps:									
1. ➔ Identify bad mood	2. ➔ Rate mood	3. ➔ Identify trigger event	4. ➔ Re-rate (or re-identify) mood	5. ➔ Identify automatic negative thoughts	6. ➔ Rate belief in negative thoughts	7 ➔ Identify cognitive distor-tions	8. ➔ Create a new rational response	9. ➔ Re-rate mood	10. Re-rate belief in original negative thought
				1.	1.	1.	1.		
				2.	2.	2.	2.		
				3.	3.	3.	3.		
				4.	4.	4.	4.		

Step 1. Identify the bad mood or negative feeling. Describe it. Depressed, angry, irritable, etc. Make sure that it is a feeling (something that you feel inside your body) not a thought in your mind.

Step 2. Rate the mood. How strong is the mood or feeling? Rate the bad mood or feelings from 0 (very least) to 100 (very most).

Step 3. Identify the trigger event. What is bothering you? Sometimes you may not know right away. But if you go over recent events in your mind, you'll probably remember an event or something that bothered you (and is probably still bothering you). Think about what negative trigger events have happened recently. Did you have an argument? Were you disappointed by something that didn't work out? Did someone say something that hurt your feelings? Describe the event or situation.

Step 4. Re-rate your negative feelings. Now that you are clear about the triggering event, look at your negative mood and feelings again. Rate how strongly you now feel the mood or negative feeling. Also, did you identify the feeling correctly? For example, instead of "anger" you may realize that your mood is better described as "hurt" or "guilt." Write down the negative mood or feeling. Once again, rate the strength of the negative feeling from 1 (very least) to 100 (very most).

Step 5. Identify the negative thoughts. Write down the negative thoughts that you had about the event or situation. List them as 1, 2, 3, and so on.

Step 6. Rate belief in negative thoughts. Rate how strongly you believe each negative thought from 1 (very least) to 100 (very most).

Step 7. Identify cognitive distortions. Look at your list of cognitive distortions from Workbook #1, Chapter 2. Figure out which negative thought is which type of cognitive distortion. Is it "all or nothing," "exaggerating," "mind reading," "trashing the positive," or what? Write down the type of cognitive distortion.

Step 8. Create a new rational idea. In the column 8, create a new idea that is more positive and realistic. Challenge each negative thought in column 5. Is it really true or is it just your opinion? Are there any facts to support the idea? Any facts that reject the idea? Where did you learn that? Now create an alternative idea that is more accurate, realistic and rational.

Step 9. Re-rate your mood. Now using the 0 to 100 scale, again rate the strength of the starting negative mood in column 2 from 1 (very least) to 100 (very most).

Step 10. Re-rate belief in first negative thoughts. Rate how strongly you now believe each of the negative thoughts you started with in column 5 from 1 (very least) to 100 (very most). Compare the rating in column 6 with the rating in column 10. You should see a reduction. You might even see a huge reduction.

These instructions will help you to complete the mood changing charts on the next two pages.

After you finish the worksheet, look over your results. What happened to your bad mood? Do you feel better when you believe in your rational thoughts rather than your negative thoughts?

Remember, this is a method you can use over and over when you find yourself "in a bad mood." You have the power to change your own bad moods into more positive feelings and a growing sense of self-pride and self-esteem.

Using Positive Thinking to Get Rid of Bad Moods – Worksheet (1)									
1.	2.	3.	4.	5.	6.	7.	8.	9.	10.
Identify bad mood	Rate mood 1-10	Identify trigger event	Re-rate (or re-identify) mood	Identify negative thoughts	Rate belief in negative thoughts 1-10	Identify cognitive distor-tions	New rational response	Re-rate mood 1-10	Re-rate belief in original negative thought
				1.			1.		
				2.			2.		
				3.			3.		
				1.			1.		
				2.			2.		
				3.			3.		

Using Positive Thinking to Get Rid of Bad Moods – Worksheet (2)									
1.	2.	3.	4.	5.	6.	7.	8.	9.	10.
Identify bad mood	Rate mood 1-10	Identify trigger event	Re-rate (or re-identify) mood	Identify negative thoughts	Rate belief in negative thoughts 1-10	Identify cognitive distortions	New rational response	Re-rate mood 1-10	Re-rate belief in original negative thought
				1.			1.		
				2.			2.		
				3.			3.		
				1.			1.		
				2.			2.		
				3.			3.		

Have Your Beliefs Put You In a Box?

Charlie felt stuck in treatment. Even though he learned that he could trust other people, he still believed that "You can't trust anyone." He could see this belief was an "all or nothing" type of cognitive distortion. He could create rational responses that disproved his own belief. But he still hung onto the old belief that he could not trust anyone. He wanted to think differently, but he couldn't seem to change his negative belief.

How about you? What beliefs do you still hold onto that keep you stuck in a box? Do you still believe something about yourself or other people or the world that makes you feel badly and act badly, but you just can't let it go of it? Rate how strongly you believe each negative belief from 1 (very least) to 10 (very most).

Rating:	Beliefs:
________	____
________	____
________	____
________	____
________	____
________	____
________	____
________	____
________	____
________	____
________	____
________	____
________	____
________	____
________	____
________	____

Getting Out of the Negative Belief Box

It might seem odd, but one big reason that people hold onto negative beliefs is that there seem to be "advantages" to negative thinking. For example, why would a smart person want to believe that he is stupid? One advantage is that he doesn't have to study harder and risk failure. If he really tried to study and got a bad grade, he is afraid he would feel even worse. Another advantage is habit. He may feel more comfortable playing the fool than showing his intelligence.

Of course, if you think about it, the "advantages" of holding onto a negative belief are usually not advantages at all. The purpose of this exercise is to help you think clearly about the advantages and disadvantages of holding onto a negative belief.

Look at the following example of a person who could not stop believing that he was ugly. Even though he was a decent-looking guy, he continued to believe he was ugly. When he sat down and really looked hard at the advantages and disadvantages of believing he was ugly, he was finally able to get out of his negative box.

My negative belief is… "I am so ugly I should feel ashamed."	
Advantages of KEEPING My negative belief	Advantages of REJECTING my negative belief
If I'm ugly, I don't have to risk getting shot down if I ask someone out on a date. If I believe I'm ugly, my loneliness won't seem so bad because I'll have a reason for being alone. If I'm ugly, I don't need to make any effort to dress well or improve myself in any way. If I'm ugly, it gives me an excuse for forcing sex from people that could reject me. I can blame all my problems on being ugly and then I won't be responsible for changing myself. If I'm ugly, I don't need to expect much from life, so I don't have to get my hopes up and risk being disappointed and feeling even worse.	If I believe that I am not ugly, I won't feel so bad about myself all the time. If I'm not ugly, I won't be afraid to approach people. If I'm not ugly, I can stand tall and proud. If I'm not ugly, I am a person worthy of respect and love. If I'm not ugly, I can have attractive friends and dates. If I'm not ugly, I can enjoy attracting attention. If I'm not ugly, I don't have to avoid people and feel so lonely and hopeless. If I'm not ugly, I will be free to develop friends and close relationships. If I'm not ugly, I don't have to live my life in one long bad mood. If I'm not ugly, I'll be able to really show what I can do.

Look at the beliefs in your Negative Belief Box (page 16). Pick a negative belief that you believe more than 50%. Use this worksheet to help yourself to get out of the Negative Belief Box. Take your time. Think of as many advantages as you can for keeping and rejecting the negative belief.

My negative belief is… ________________________________	
Advantages of KEEPING My negative belief	Advantages of REJECTING my negative belief

Go back through the list of "advantages." Which ones, if any, are advantages? Is there anything you can think of that would weaken or destroy that "advantage"?

Now re-rate the strength of your belief in the negative belief. Do you see a reduction in the strength of the negative belief? Do you see an increase in positive thinking?

Create an "advantages" worksheet for other negative beliefs that were rated greater than 50% and go through this method of getting out of the negative belief box.

CHAPTER 9
SUBSTANCE ABUSE AND ACTING OUT

Beliefs About Substance Abuse Questionnaire

This is a list of some common beliefs about using drugs and alcohol. Please read each statement and rate how much you agree or disagree with each one.

1	2	3	4	5	6	7
Totally Disagree	Disagree Very Much	Disagree Slightly	Neutral	Agree Slightly	Agree Very Much	Totally Agree

____ 1. Life without using drugs or alcohol is boring.
____ 2. Using is the only way to increase my creativity and productivity.
____ 3. I can't function without drugs/alcohol.
____ 4. This is the only way to cope with the pain in my life.
____ 5. I'm not ready to stop using.
____ 6. The cravings and urges make me use.
____ 7. My life won't get any better, even if I stop using.
____ 8. The only way to deal with my anger is by using.
____ 9. Life would be depressing if I stopped.
____ 10. I don't deserve to recover from drug use.
____ 11. I'm not a strong enough person to stop.
____ 12. I could not be comfortable with other people without using.
____ 13. Substance use is not a problem for me.
____ 14. The cravings and urges won't go away unless I use drugs.
____ 15. My substance use is caused by someone else (friends, family, etc.).
____ 16. If someone has a problem with drugs, it's all genetic.
____ 17. I can't relax without drugs.
____ 18. Having this drug problem means I am a bad person.
____ 19. I can't control my anxiety without using drugs.
____ 20. I can't make my life fun unless I use.

Aaron Beck: Cognitive Therapy with Substance Abuse

Craving Beliefs Questionnaire

This is a list of some common beliefs about using drugs and alcohol. Please read each statement and rate how much you agree or disagree with each one.

1	2	3	4	5	6	7
Totally Disagree	Disagree Very Much	Disagree Slightly	Neutral	Agree Slightly	Agree Very Much	Totally Agree

____ 1. The craving is a physical reaction therefore, I can't do anything about it.

____ 2. If I don't use, the cravings will get worse.

____ 3. Craving can drive you crazy.

____ 4. The craving makes me use drugs.

____ 5. I'll always have cravings for drugs.

____ 6. I don't have any control over the craving.

____ 7. Once the craving starts, I have no control over my behavior.

____ 8 I'll have cravings for drugs the rest of my life

____ 9. I can't stand the physical symptoms I have while craving drugs.

____ 10. The craving is my punishment for using drugs.

____ 11. If you have never used drugs then you have no idea what the craving is like (and you can't expect me to resist).

____ 12. The images/thoughts I have while craving drugs are out of my control.

____ 13. The craving makes me so nervous I can't stand it.

____ 14. I'll never be prepared to handle the craving.

____ 15. Since I'll have the craving the rest of my life, I might as well go ahead and use drugs.

____ 16. When I'm really craving drugs, I can't function.

____ 17. Either I'm strongly craving drugs or I'm not; there is nothing in between.

____ 18. If the craving gets too intense, using drugs is the only way to cope with the feeling.

____ 19. When craving drugs, it's OK to use alcohol to cope.

____ 20. The craving is stronger than my willpower.

Aaron Beck: Cognitive Therapy with Substance Abuse

Relapse Prediction Scale

A relapse is when you begin to engage in your destructive behavior again. In this case relapse refers to using alcohol or drugs again. There are many situations that can trigger an urge to use drugs or alcohol. Here is a list of some situations that might trigger strong urges to use drugs or drink alcohol. Read each item and imagine yourself in that situation. In the first column, "Strength of Urges," predict how strong you think the urge will be to use drugs or alcohol if you are in that situation. In the second column, "Likelihood of Using," predict how likely it will be that you will use drugs or alcohol if you are in that situation.

0	1	2	3	4
None	Weak	Moderate	Strong	Very Strong

	Prediction	
	Strength of urges	Likelihood of using
1. I am in a place where I used alcohol or other drugs before.		
2. I am around people with whom I used drugs and alcohol in the past.		
3. I just got some money.		
4. I see my peers using drugs and alcohol.		
5. I am leaving work or school.		
6. It's Friday night.		
7. I am at a party.		
8. I am thinking about the last time I used.		
9. I start talking with someone about using.		
10. I feel bored.		
11. I feel great!		
12. I see my romantic partner.		
13. I am having a drink.		
14. My friend is offering me some alcohol or drugs.		
15. I feel sad.		
16. I see a previous partner.		
17. I am out looking for sex.		
18. I feel sexy.		
19. I remember how good the high feels.		
20. I feel angry.		

	Prediction	
	Strength of urges	Likelihood of using
21. I feel stressed out.		
22. I feel guilty.		
23. I just used drugs or drank alcohol.		
24. I just relapsed.		
25. I am getting ready for work or school.		
26. I am tired.		
27. I am frustrated.		
28. I see an anti-drug use poster.		
29. I see a pipe.		
30. I am stealing.		
31. I just had a dream about using or drinking.		
32. I am watching sports.		
33. I am getting dressed up.		
34. I am under pressure at school.		
35. I am thinking about having sex.		
36. I am angry at my romantic partner.		
37. My romantic partner is bugging me about my using.		
38. My family is bugging me about my using.		
39. I was just told I have a positive urine.		
40. I didn't use, yet my urine was positive.		
41. I am watching a drug-related movie or video games with drug scenes.		
42. I feel anxious.		
43. Someone just criticized me.		
44. I haven't used for a long time.		
45. I feel pressure at my job.		
46. Someone I care for is ill or dying.		
47. I am in pain.		
48. I feel a burden on my shoulders.		
49. I am at a party having a good time.		
50. I had a fight with my family.		

Aaron Beck: Cognitive Therapy with Substance Abuse

The Role of Drugs and Alcohol in Abusing

There are many ways that drugs and alcohol play a role in abuses. Some might be obvious. Some are not. Go through the checklist and put a "√" by the statements that are true for you.

	1. When I get high or drunk, it puts me in the mood for acting out.
	2. Drinking or using drugs makes me feel more confident to do what I want to do.
	3. Getting drunk or high helps to take away any guilt or bad feelings that I might have about committing a crime or hurting someone.
	4. If my victim was drunk or high, it makes it easier to take advantage of my victim.
	5. Drinking or using drugs makes me feel more relaxed so I can better enjoy myself.
	6. Drugs and alcohol help me to get wild and I like getting wild.
	7. Drinking or getting high makes me less afraid of getting caught for a crime.
	8. If I am drunk or high when I act out, I can tell myself later that it wasn't my fault. It only happened because I was stoned.
	9. If I'm drunk or high, I don't have to think about tomorrow and the consequences of what I'm doing.
	10. Drugs and alcohol help me to forget my pain.
	11. Drugs and alcohol give me a reason to claim that I don't remember doing anything wrong.
	12. Drugs and alcohol help me to forget the bad things I have done to others.
	13. I feel better about myself when I'm drinking or using drugs.

Negative Beliefs in Substance Abuse and Acting Out

The negative belief patterns of acting out and substance abuse are similar. When a person has deep negative thoughts about himself, it tends to feed negative moods and negative behavior that hurts himself/herself and others. The key is to get at those deep-set negative beliefs that feed the bad behavior. For example, a person may believe that, "I am trapped. I feel bad. There's nothing I can do to get out of my situation." This negative belief leads to another negative belief that, "The only way I can feel better or escape my situation is to get high."

Look at the examples on the left column, then think about how negative beliefs apply to you and your use of drugs or alcohol. Put your answers in the blanks on the right.

Negative beliefs about self	Negative beliefs about myself
Examples: I am trapped. I am a jerk. No one could ever love a creep like me. ↓	↓
Trigger urges and thoughts about using drugs and alcohol	My trigger urges and thoughts about using drugs and alcohol
Examples: I won't feel so bad if I get high. It will be fun to get high. The only way I can feel good is to get stoned. I deserve a little pleasure. ↓	↓
Trigger thoughts to give myself permission to get high	Trigger thoughts to give self permission to get high
Examples: I will feel better if I do this. I will escape from my problems. Everybody else does it.	

Questions About Using Substances and Acting Out

In order to change unhealthy beliefs about getting drunk and high, it is important to get a clear understanding of how these beliefs affect your life. Answer each of the following questions.

What types of drugs and alcohol have you used to get high? What have you used most often? ____________________

____

____

How do you feel when you use drugs and/or alcohol? ____________________

____

____

____

How often have you combined drugs and alcohol? If you have combined drugs and alcohol to get high, how did it make you feel? ____________________

____

____

____

Do you feel stronger or more confident when you use drugs and/or alcohol? If yes, explain what that is like for you. ____________________

____

____

____

In what ways do you act differently or see things differently when you are using drugs or alcohol? ____________________

____

____

____

How often were you under the influence of drugs and/or alcohol when you committed your abuse(s)? Describe how this worked for you. ______________________________

____

____

____

____

Have you had regrets about using drugs or alcohol because of what you did while you were high or drunk? When and why? ______________________________

____

____

____

Do you feel better when you are high or drunk than when you are not? If yes, why do you think that is so? ______________________________

____

____

____

Since you started using drugs and/or alcohol, what is the longest time you have gone without using? ______________________________

____

____

____

If you could not use drugs and alcohol, what would you do instead? Describe how your daily life would be different without drinking or using drugs. ______________________________

____

____

____

What are the disadvantages of using drugs and alcohol? Think about what you have suffered or lost because of your use of substances. ____________________

____

____

____

What else can you do to get what you want without offending or using drugs or alcohol?

____

____

____

____

Now look back over your answers to the previous questions. Examine your thoughts and beliefs using what you've learned about cognitive distortions. Do you find that many of your ideas are cognitive distortions? How can you use what you've learned to test the beliefs and think about healthy rational alternative beliefs? ________________

____

____

____

Based on the work of Aaron Beck in Cognitive Therapy with Substance Abuse

Advantages and Disadvantages Box

This exercise will help you to stay clear about how the many disadvantages of abusing drugs and alcohol always outweigh the few advantages.

	Using Drugs and/or Alcohol	Not Using Drugs and/or Alcohol
ADVANTAGES		
DISADVANTAGES		

Go back over the reasons for not using drugs and alcohol. Pick the three strongest reasons that matter to you. Then get a small card and write them on a small card that you can carry with you. The next time you feel an urge for drinking or using drugs, read the card.

Do You Have Low Frustration Tolerance?

You may have a "low frustration tolerance." This simply means that you get upset over many different things and you are easily frustrated by things that are not very important. You are not able to "tolerate" (handle) little annoying events without upset. You may notice that you often get bothered by things that don't seem to upset other people.

This is a way to test your frustration tolerance. Mark a "√" to show if the statement is "often" true for you, "sometimes" true for you, or "not me."

often	sometimes	not me	
			If I want something, I must have it immediately.
			If I have to wait for what I want or someone gets in my way, I get very upset.
			If I am frustrated in one situation, I often over-generalize and say things "always" go badly for me or "never" go the way I want them to.
			I feel like anything that goes wrong is directed against me personally and doesn't cause a problem for other people.
			I feel like the world owes me what I want. I feel entitled to get what I want.
			If things don't go the way I planned or if I can't get what I want, I act like it's a great disaster or catastrophe.
			When other people don't follow my rules or do what I want, I just want to give up and quit.
			I feel entitled to be angry at anything that people do if I believe it shows me disrespect.
			When I can't get what I want, I feel like I'm a helpless victim or a failure or that no one can love me.
			I let my anger build and build and then I punish the person who did me wrong.
			The best way for me to handle my anger and fear is to use drugs or alcohol.
			I hate it when other people get in my way.
			When I fail at something, I think it proves that I am a loser.
			When I can't get what I want, I hate myself.

Based on the work of Aaron Beck in Cognitive Therapy with Substance Abuse.

Cognitive Distortions Cause Low Frustration Tolerance

As you may have guessed, "low frustration tolerance" is caused by cognitive distortions. Look back over the test and pick out the four items that are most upsetting for you. Enter them in the chart below and complete the exercise.

Negative belief (from previous page)	Rate belief 1 to 10	Identify Cognitive Distortions	Create a new rational alternative	Rate new belief 1 to 10

Chapter 10
Victime Empathy

Post Traumatic Stress Disorder

Victims of abuse go through a series of very painful experiences. There are painful effects at the time of the abuse, more painful effects as the victim tries to recover from the abuse, and more painful long-term effects that can haunt the victim for the rest of his or her life. This is called "post traumatic stress disorder" (PTSD).

Victims of abuse go through three periods of adjustment – immediate, intermediate and long-term. Each period has a set of painful problems.

IMMEDIATE IMPACT – First period of extreme upset and disorganization:

- Feeling powerless or having no control over one's life.
- Extreme fear or terror or panic – especially when exposed to events or situations that remind her/him of the abuse/trauma.
- Feels shame and guilt.
- Wide range of emotions – two types of reactions:
  Blunted emotion: victim feels dazed, stunned, in shock, numb or dead inside.
  Extreme emotion: sudden extreme emotions and sharp changes in emotions.
- Mood swings – sudden crying spells, outbursts of rage, irritable, agitated.
- Unable to think clearly, unable to concentrate.
- Unable to sleep.
- Unable to eat.
- Physical problems, like stomach aches, headaches, digestion, etc.
- Thinking over and over and over about the events of the abuse.
- Reactions that seem way too extreme for the event.
- Fear of never recovering – despair and hopelessness.
- Dissociation (feeling like you are outside of yourself or separated from yourself).
- Flashbacks – terrifying memories or nightmares about the abuse.

- Difficulty with remembering things, especially things related to the trauma.
- Feeling "scattered" and confused, unable to make decisions.
- Feeling disoriented, like you are not yourself.
- Dreading the future and expecting bad things to happen.
- Unable to enjoy normal lifestyle.

INTERMEDIATE IMPACT: Second period of struggling to adjust:

- The intermediate period may last from several weeks to several years.
- Victim tries to pull her/himself together and get back to normal life.
- Struggles to get over the trauma – often by minimizing or denying the full pain and impact of the abuse.
- Victim restricts her/his feelings and perceptions in order to avoid reminders of the trauma.
- Feels numb emotionally.
- Continues to feel shame and guilt.
- Disconnected from family and friends and activities, withdraws into isolation.
- Easily scared or startled, is edgy, and overly alert.
- Over-protective of loved ones and extremely fearful for their safety.
- Super-alert, always expecting danger.
- Needs to control every detail of everyday issues.
- Does not want to burden others with her/his problems.
- Difficulty trusting loved ones or other people, fears betrayal.
- Increased use of alcohol or drugs.
- Negative changes in personality.
- Worries about recovering.
- Unable to enjoy normal lifestyle.

LONG-TERM IMPACT: Third period of trying to get back to normal:

- Depression, sadness, no energy to do anything.
- Irrational fears and phobias.
- Continuing physical problems, like stomach aches, headaches, digestion, etc.
- Problems with sleeping, nightmares.
- Changes in routine.
- Stress on relationships, marital problems, family problems.
- Unable to enjoy normal lifestyle.
- Continues to feel shame and guilt, including blaming self and survivor guilt.
- Flashbacks and nightmares about the abuse.
- Lacks a sense of order, fairness and safety in the world.

Important Facts to Know About Victims of Sexual and Other Abuse

1. Both victims and abusers use cognitive distortions to deal with most abuse, especially the following:
   - Minimizing – pretending that whatever happened was not as bad as it was.
   - Rationalizing – try to explain it away.
   - Denying – pretending that what is happening *isn't* or that whatever happened *didn't*.
   - Justifying – making what happened sound reasonable and acceptable.

2. How do victims and abusers differ in their use of cognitive distortions?
   - Abusers: Use cognitive distortions to allow themselves to continue abusing.
   - Victims: Use cognitive distortions as a way of trying to handle their victimization.

3. Other ways that victims of abuse may try to handle their victimization:
   - Forgetting (repression) – pushing the abuse out of awareness and memory.
   - Splitting – feeling as if one is divided into more than one person; numbing one's body so as not to feel the pain; or leaving one's body and watching the abuse as from a distance.
   - Control – trying to stay in control of every aspect of one's life.
   - Escaping through distractions – such as drinking, using drugs, gambling, working too much, keeping too busy, running away, reading, getting sick, living in chaos, and other problems.
   - Self-destructive behaviors – such as cutting or hurting oneself (which puts the victim in control of the pain rather than the abuser); and suicide attempts (suicide appears to the victim as the only way out of the pain of the abuse).
   - Avoiding closeness – protecting oneself against hurt by not allowing loved ones or others to get close.
   - Being obsessed with sex – either doing everything possible to avoid sex, or always seeking sex.

4. A child victim of sexual, physical and emotional abuse can be damaged in many ways, including:
   - Unable to be close – the victim may be unable to trust anyone; may repeatedly test people to be sure they can be trusted; may get involved with bad relationships and abusive people; may not be able to give and receive affection.
   - Poor self-esteem – the victim may feel different, dirty, powerless, worthless.
   - Emotional confusion – the victim may be unable to recognize, express, or value feelings and emotions.

- Negative feelings about one's body – the victim may feel like he/she is outside his/her own body; may take poor care of his/her body and health; may do self-destructive things such as cutting or hurting oneself.
- Sexual problems – the victim may try to use sex to meet other non-sexual needs; may "numb out" or panic when having sex; may need to control every detail of sex in order to feel safe.
- Problems with parenting – the victim may abuse his/her own children or avoid children for fear of being abusive.
- Poor family relationships – the victim of incest may feel crazy or depressed around family; may feel unsafe around the family; may cut self off from family members.

5. Most healthy people believe that there is law and order in the world, that most people can be trusted, that they are safe in their homes, and that they have some control over the events in their lives. When a person is sexually abused and victimized, these beliefs are badly shaken or destroyed.

6. The pain of victimization is both physical and emotional. The emotional wounds are even more painful and long lasting than physical wounds.

7. Many victims of sexual abuse suffer from Post-Traumatic Stress Disorder (PTSD). PTSD begins with an extremely upsetting event, such as a plane crash, earthquake, or sexual assault and can last for months, years, or even a lifetime. PTSD for victims of sexual abuse includes the following upset:
   - Re-living the abuse over and over in the form of nightmares, bad memories, and flashbacks.
   - Feeling extremely upset when faced with things related to the abuse, such as a particular place, person, date, situation, etc.
   - Avoiding things related to the abuse, such as avoiding sex, losing interest in important life activities, avoiding places or situations that remind the victim of the abuse.
   - Feeling numb inside – The victim feels numb or dead inside or has very little feeling. The victim may feel cut off from feelings or from his/her body.
   - Being super-alert to danger, such as being easily startled, unable to fall or stay asleep, unable to relax and feel safe, unable to concentrate, and feeling edgy and irritable.

8. Sexual abuse and sexual violence changes the way victims think about themselves, the opposite sex, and their sexual behavior. For example, victims may start to see sex as a way of getting power or control or as a way to hurt or punish other people. Or victims

may start to see themselves as dirty or worthless sex objects. Or victims may be frightened and distrustful of persons of the opposite sex.

9. Sexually abusing others is not just about sex. It is more about wanting to control, dominate, punish and terrify another person. Most of the time, sexual abuse is more about anger and violence than sexual pleasure.

About Rape:

There are many myths about rape that are sometimes believed, but are NOT true:

- Abuse is sex. – No! Abuse is more about violence than sex. The rapist wants to have total control over his victim by using terror and shame. The rapist wants to feel strong and powerful by making his victim feel weak and helpless. He wants to degrade, shame and hurt his victim.
- Men are driven to abuse by lust. – No! Rapists are not just hungry for sex. Rapists use abuse to express anger and to feel powerful. They use the feeling of power as a way to get more turned on.
- Rapists are loners. – No! Rapists can be just about anybody, including men who are married, popular, rich, or seen as leaders in the community.
- Women make men want to abuse. – No! Victims do not do things that make men want to abuse them. Abuse victims can be of any age, race, dress, or class. The abuse victims at one hospital ranged in age from two months to 97 years. Abuse victims can be young or old, male or female, black or white, thin or fat, short or tall, wearing make-up or not wearing make-up, wearing skirts or wearing pants, wearing long skirts or short skirts, and so on.
- Only bad women are abused. – No! The victim's character or behavior does not have anything to do with being abused. Women do not cause men to want to abuse them. Men decide.

Child Sexual Abuse:

Child sexual abuse is terribly harmful for many reasons, including:

- Traumatic sexualization – When children are sexually abused, they feel things in their body that are very upsetting and confusing. They are too young to know what the feelings are or what to do with them. The sensations from the sexual abuse can be painful, confusing, stimulating, embarrassing and terrifying, and children do not know how to handle these sensations. The confused feelings can distort the child's growing self-image and his/her understanding of relationships and behavior. (Remember, there is no such thing as "appropriate" sexual stimulation that can be done to children!)
- "Damaged Goods" – The victim has a shameful feeling of being "damaged" by the sexual abuse. If family members and peers do not believe the victim or pretend it did

not happen, or blame the victim for the molestation, the victim feels even more shame, guilt, and self-hatred.

- Betrayal – When a child victim is abused and manipulated by a trusted caretaker (like a parent, uncle, teacher, scout leader, priest, etc.), it makes it extremely hard for the child to trust people in the future, especially loved ones.
- Helplessness – The victim feels helpless during the sexual abuse and is unable to stop it, which leads to strong feelings of fear and helplessness.

Sexual Abuse of Children:

Eight factors determine how badly a child is harmed by sexual molestation:

- The age and maturity level of the child at the time of the abuse.
- How the abuse started, how often the child was molested, and how long the child was molested.
- The nature of the abuse (how much violence, force, or pressure was used against the child and the severity of physical damage to the child).
- Whether the abuser is a trusted loved one or a stranger.
- The strength of the victim's personality before the abuse.
- Whether the child is believed, supported and protected by family members after the abuse is discovered.
- How authorities, such as the police, lawyers, teachers, child protection services, and other agencies respond to the discovery of the sexual abuse.
- Whether the victim receives therapy to deal with the trauma of sexual abuse.

The serious damage caused to children by sexual molestation includes:

- Damaged Goods Syndrome.
- Guilt feelings for being somehow responsible for having been sexually abused; guilt about pleasurable feelings experienced as part of the sexual molestation. (Remember, the human body may respond to sexual stimulation whether the child desires it or not).
- Fearful.
- Depressed.
- Low self-esteem.
- Anger (usually hidden and not directly expressed).
- Difficulty trusting others.
- Confusion about personal boundaries – The parent is supposed to be the protector, supporter, and caretaker and the child is the one to be protected, supported and cared for. In a sexually abusive relationship, the parent may demand that the child meet his/her needs instead of caring for the child's needs. Or, the child may become a protector by not telling about the abuse.
- False maturity – After being sexually abused, some children may appear older or more mature on the surface because they are trying to handle the emotional pain and confusion on their own.

- Self-control – Molestation is a violation of the child's body, his/her sense of personal privacy, and his/her right to self-control. The child receives the message (and may start to believe) that he/she has no rights and can be used by others.

Children try to handle the pain and shame of sexual molestation by:

- Keeping it secret – Most victims do not disclose the sexual abuse.
- Delayed and unconvincing disclosure – Because of strong fears and mixed emotions, victims often delay telling about the sexual abuse, and when they do tell, they are often not very convincing.
- Changing stories – Disclosing the sexual abuse can cause a storm of events that are frightening and upsetting for the child – seeing upset parents, angry parents, police, doctors, child protection investigators, etc. Unfortunately, for some victims, it is safer and less painful to take their story back and pretend to be a liar rather than deal with the fall-out of telling the truth about the abuse.

My Commitment to Learning Empathy

Empathy means truly understanding the thoughts, feelings and behaviors of another person and then acting on that understanding in a caring way. It is "walking in the other person's shoes." The opposite is to be cold and uncaring.

All abusers have a lack of empathy for the victim at the time of the abuse. If you are serious about never abusing again, you must face your lack of empathy and begin to change it. Read each of the following facts and then sign your name as a sign of your commitment to learning empathy and taking responsibility:

1. Although I am not evil, I have done very bad things that have hurt others and I was wrong to do what I did.

   ____

   signature and date

2. I hurt other people because I was selfish and it was my decision to hurt others as a way of dealing with my emotional needs and problems.

   ____

   signature and date

3. Even if I suffered physical, emotional or sexual abuse myself, it is never an excuse for committing abuse against others. My own victimization may have played a part in my decision to abuse, but it was still my decision. Many victims choose a healthy lifestyle and never choose to hurt anyone else. Being a victim of any kind of abuse is never an excuse for hurting someone else.

   ____

   signature and date

4. I can learn how to handle situations, relate to people, and meet my emotional needs in ways that do not hurt other people.

____

signature and date

5. Learning to relate to others and meeting my needs without hurting other people is not easy, but it is rewarding. It will maintain my good standing in the community, raise my self-esteem, and help me to build healthy relationships.

____

signature and date

6. Learning empathy for the feelings of others, and changing my behavior accordingly, is part of learning to relate to others and learning to meet my needs without hurting someone else.

____

signature and date

Factors That Increase Damage to Molested Children*

Sexual molestation can cause severe harm to children, including physical, emotional, social and mental damage. In addition, there are factors that can make the damage even worse.

1. The child experienced some sexual responsiveness during the molestation/abuse.

   Facts:
   - The human body works from birth, including the sexual organs.
   - Causing children to have a sexual response is extremely damaging.
   - Sexual abuse can "train" a child to be aroused by the abuse and this can carry into adulthood.

2. The sexual abuse used terror and terror building.

   Facts:
   - If the child must wait in fear for the expected sexual abuse or is subject to repeated and ritualistic abuse, it creates a painful and degrading sense of anticipation.
   - The abuser can terrorize a child without using violence, weapons, or physical damage. The threat or perceived threat of harm is enough to create terror.

3. The child is manipulated to *not* see the abuser as an abuser.

   Facts:
   - When the abuser has some positive characteristics in the victim's mind (like a parent or loved one), the child victim cannot recognize the abuser as being abusive and responsible for his actions.
   - The abuser may create situations where the victim is manipulated into pleasing the abuser or seeking love and acceptance from the abuser.
   - The abuser may create situations where surviving the abuse was connected to pleasing the abuser or being close to the abuser.
   - If the abuser is highly regarded by community or by people close to the victim, it is difficult for the victim to see the abuser as an abuser.

4. The victim is manipulated to *not* see him/herself as a victim of abuse.

   Facts:
   - Emotional damage occurs when the victim cannot view him/herself as an innocent child who has been robbed of something precious.
   - Abusers manipulate the victim into feeling responsible for being abused. "I wouldn't do this to you if I didn't know you wanted it."

**Information is based on Just Before Dawn (1989) by Jan Hindman.*

- When the abuser makes the child feel like a willing partner, it causes the victim to feel guilty, dirty, and bad.
- Abusers often pick child victims who are already struggling with poor self-esteem and are more likely to accept blame for the abuse.

5. The younger the child, the worse the damage.

   Facts:
   - Younger children have more stages of life to pass through than older children. Each stage of life can add to the trauma and present more abuse issues for the child to struggle with.
   - Young children are less able to make sense of the sexual abuse.

6. The child reacts to the abuse with memory impairment or self-abuse.

   Facts:
   - Children try to deal with the pain and shame of something that is sexual abuse in different ways.
   - Many victims may deny, rationalize, justify, and minimize their abuse to attempt to avoid the painful reality.
   - Two kinds of reactions can cause on-going, severe damage:
     - ✦ Memory damage– Amnesia (total lack of recall) or dissociation (separating awareness of abuse and pain from other parts of awareness) can cause memory gaps. Later, as adults, victims may have dim memories or odd feelings, which do not seem to make sense, causing the victim to feel crazy or out of control.
     - ✦ Self-abuse patterns – Victims may match their inner sense of being bad and dirty through self-destructive acts, such as sexual promiscuity, substance abuse, criminal behavior, eating disorders, suicide attempts and other symbolic "bad" behavior.

7. The sexual abuse was kept secret.

   Facts:
   - Children, who are unable to report the sexual abuse, may spend much of their lives suffering in silence, feeling guilty or bad.
   - The child is unable to build a healthy sense of sexuality on a foundation of guilt, shame, pain, confusion and the abusive experiences caused by the sex abuser.

8. Disclosing the sexual abuse results in bad consequences for the victim.

   Facts:
   - Far greater trauma is caused when the reaction to the victim's disclosure is negative, such as calling the child a liar, blaming the child for breaking up the family, or blaming the child for the abuse.
   - Negative responses to the disclosure of abuse may lead to beatings, threats, abuse, public shame, being sent away, family break-ups, abandonment by the family, or other negative outcomes.

9. Continuing contact between the victim and abuser.

   Facts:
   - Greater damage occurs when the victim must have continuing contact with the abuser or with people close to the abuser because the victim is constantly reminded of the sexual abuse and abuser.
   - This is especially traumatic when the abuser is valued more than the victim or the abuser is more respected by family and the community.

Empathy Exercises

Given what you have learned about the pain and lasting impact of abuse on victims, write a detailed report of what it is like to be the victim of your abuse. Write a description of what it is like to be victimized in the first person – that is, use "I" rather than "he" or "she" when describing the experience. Respond to the following questions:

1) Write as though you are your victim and the abuse is happening to you now. Write how the victim is feeling as the abuse is being committed. It is not enough to write, "she/he may have felt bad." Instead describe the feelings and emotions such as, "I am afraid," or "What is happening?!"

2) Write about your victim's experience after the abuse.

   a) What did your victim experience as he/she reported the abuse? Who did he/she tell first and how do you think your victim felt after having to repeat the story of the abuse to police, social services, etc.

   b) Describe your victim's experiences in the court process. How did he/she feel having to describe the abuse to the judge, prosecutor, defense attorney, and witnesses?

3) Your abusive behavior did not end when you walked away, or when you were convicted. Write about the long-term effects of your abuse on your victim.

4) How did your victim's family and friends react to your abuse?

5) Write a letter of responsibility to your victim, **not to be mailed**. Upon completing the letter, have another group member read the letter as you, while you listen and respond as your **victim**.

Waves From A Pebble

Just as a pebble tossed into a pond causes rings of waves to ripple outward in all directions, abuse has a wide impact on the lives of many other people. Abuse not only harms the victim, it can have a serious negative effect on the victim's family, friends, neighbors, community and others. The diagram below shows how abuse can have wide effects like the waves from a pebble.

Exercise: Starting in the center and working outward think about ALL the people whose lives have been affected by your abusive behavior. You may have to think deeply about this. List as many people as you can think of. Starting with the victim, think about the impact on the victim's immediate family (spouse, children), primary family (parents, siblings), extended family (aunts, uncles, in-laws), friends and neighbors, legal personnel (lawyer, courts) and others. Then consider the impact on your own immediate family, primary family, extended family, friends and neighbors, and other people. You can include additional persons who are not suggested.

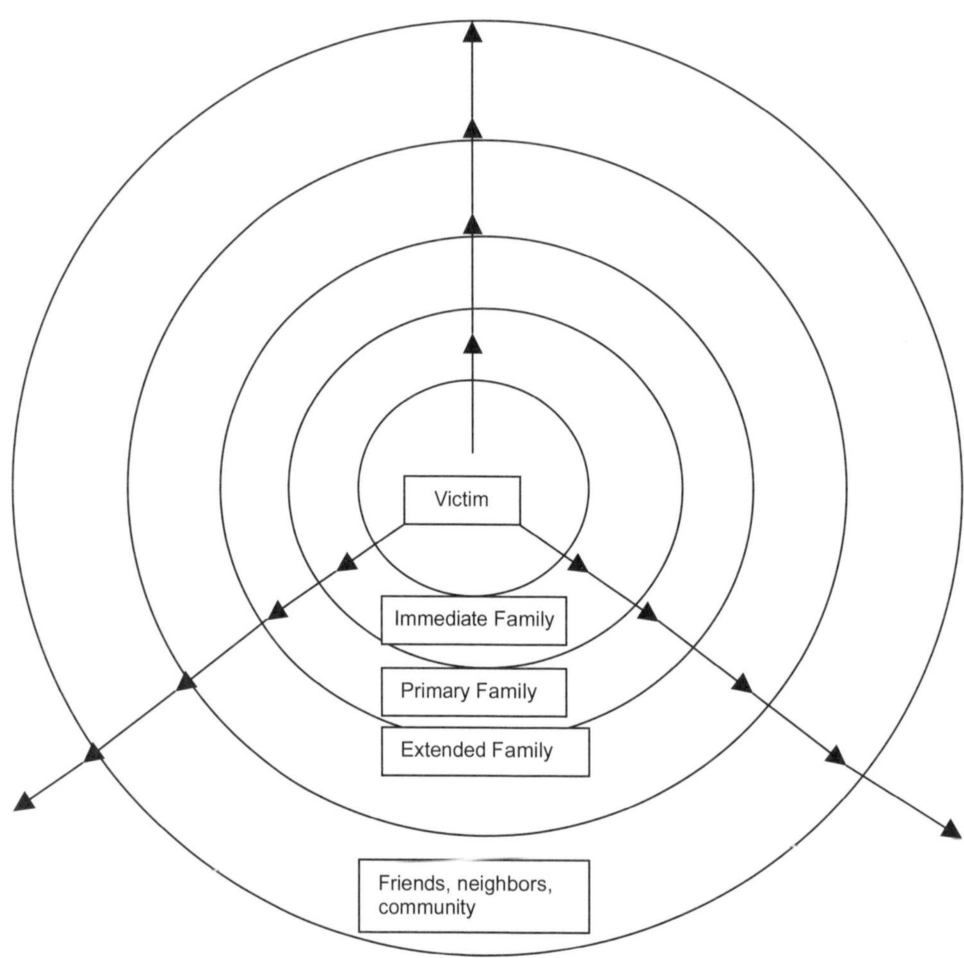

Showing Empathy With a Letter of Responsibility

Write a letter (NOT to be sent) to your victim in which you take full responsibility for the abuse that you committed and try to show that you have true empathy for the victim. Then use this checklist to go through your letter and evaluate if you have done the things you need to do to take responsibility and have true empathy.

Then write a second draft and repeat the same evaluation. Remember that it may take many drafts before you have taken full responsibility for the damage you have done.

Rating Sheet for Letter of Responsibility to Your Victim	
	1. You apologize – say you are sorry for what you've done.
	2. You take responsibility for your own actions.
	3. You do not justify your actions. You make no excuses and do not give "reasons" for what you've done. You do not minimize the damage.
	4. You do not blame the victim or shift blame to other people or circumstances.
	5. You explain why your behavior was inappropriate and wrong.
	6. You do NOT describe any events, words or actions related to the abuse that could be painful or embarrassing to the victim.
	7. You accept that your punishment is deserved, but that your suffering is not as bad as the suffering of the victim.
	8. You state that you have caused great pain, suffering and harm to the victim.
	9. You state that your abuse has also hurt many other people in addition to the victim (ripple effect on family, friends, neighbors, etc.).
	10. You explain that the victim's anger is totally justified.
	11. You do not give advice to the victim or use words to control the victim's feelings or reactions.
	12. You do not put the spotlight on yourself or your own feelings or suffering.
	13. You do not feel sorry for yourself.
	14. You do not ask for forgiveness or show expectations of future forgiveness. Saying "I hope you can forgive me…" is more about yourself than your victim. It can make the victim feel anger or guilt for not forgiving.

Interview With Jason Victim of Sexual Abuse #1

INTERVIEWER: Can you tell me how old you are?

JASON: I am eighteen.

INTERVIEWER: And at some point you were sexually victimized?

JASON: Yes.

INTERVIEWER: How old were you when you were first sexually victimized?

JASON: The first time I was victimized, I was eight years old.

INTERVIEWER: Eight years old?

JASON: Yes, I was in a foster home and one of the foster brothers there had, well, we were out in the woods playing and we were playing with walkie-talkies and he forced me down on the ground and performed anal sex on me. The other kids that were playing with us kind of came up on it and we went and told our foster parents. He got kicked out of the house.

INTERVIEWER: Did you get any help or treatment or counseling after that?

JASON: Not for that specific incident. I was in counseling for behavior problems I had in school, but not for being offended.

INTERVIEWER: Do you remember at the time what some of your thoughts or feelings were about what had happened?

JASON: Yeah, I was hurt and I was wondering why this was happening and questioned if this kind of thing was supposed to go on. I was real confused because I was real young and I really didn't know if it was right or wrong.

INTERVIEWER: So you were confused. Were you sexually victimized at some other point?

JASON: Yeah. I stayed in that foster home for a few years and when I turned eleven I was placed up for an adoption and I was going to be adopted by a young guy. He adopted me and I went to live with him when I was about eleven years old. He had asked me to sleep in his room because my room wasn't quite finished. That is where the television was and that is where we spent most of the time... in his room. We didn't use the living room that often. I was in his room watching television and I fell asleep on the bed. In the middle of the night I kind of felt something rubbing on my backside. At first I was kind of halfway asleep. I thought about it for a second, but I really didn't think much about it... that he was trying to touch me or anything. I just thought maybe he shifted or something. So I really didn't pay it any mind, I just drifted back to sleep.

Again, the next day, the same thing happened. I was in his room and we were watching television and I fell asleep again. Again I woke up in the middle of the night and I felt something rubbing on me. This time I really knew he was rubbing his private on me. I shifted my body and pretended I was still asleep. That is when he asked me if I was still awake. I said yeah. He started asking me sexual questions. He asked me if I had ever had sex. He asked me if he could fondle me and he started to play with my private. I got aroused and he started asking me to perform anal intercourse on him. That is when I really didn't know what to do. I was really afraid because he was bigger than I was. I was eleven and was really small for my age anyway. So, I just did what he asked me to do. I did it, and after he was done, he told me that I had better not tell anybody because if I did, he would just tell my social worker that I came into his room in the middle of the night and I touched him. He said they would believe him and I would go back to a foster home.

I didn't tell anybody because I really wanted a family. I was in foster homes for awhile and it wasn't quite the same as having a family of your own. You really weren't allowed to do too much. It wasn't that the foster parents were mean to me. I just didn't have any real friends. I was allowed to play in the yard, but I didn't really have good social skills and friends and stuff. When he adopted me, I felt real special and that somebody wanted me and they were going to take care of me. That is what he told me… that he was going to take care of me. That is why I didn't tell anybody... because I didn't want to go back to foster homes. Then, later we put the television in the living room and we were in there, he was sitting on the couch and he started to touch himself and he wanted me to perform oral sex on him. I was afraid to say no. I did it and then he had me perform anal intercourse on him on the couch.

INTERVIEWER: So you were eleven when it began with your adoptive father?

JASON: Yeah. Uh huh.

INTERVIEWER: After the sexual abuse began at eleven, how old were you when it stopped?

JASON: I was sixteen.

INTERVIEWER: So for five years you were sexually abused by your adoptive father?

JASON: Yeah.

INTERVIEWER: Can you describe how it affected you during those years and what those years were like for you?

JASON: Yeah. Well, I was really depressed. I didn't know what to do. I was afraid to say anything to anybody. I had to keep those feelings inside. I didn't have anyone to turn to that I could talk to about my problems. I didn't talk to my dad about my problems or anything like that. I kept all those feelings and frustrations inside. I had problems emotionally and socially too. I didn't trust too many people because I didn't want other people to start doing it to me either (start abusing me). So I distanced myself from people when I would make friends. I would keep them for awhile and when I felt like the friendship was getting too close, I would do something to mess it up so we wouldn't be friends anymore. I started misbehaving in school and not listening to my teachers and became a problem-child in school and became very disrespectful to my teachers.

INTERVIEWER: What were your thoughts about yourself and what are some of the things you thought about yourself during those years?

JASON: I thought that somehow I deserve this and I guess it was just meant to be and I just had to try and deal with it. I didn't think I was a worthwhile person and I really felt bad. I didn't have high self-esteem... I had real low self-esteem, always downing myself. I felt angry inside. I was depressed and real sad. I just really disliked myself because after awhile I thought that I should have been able to stop what happened and that I didn't. I let it continue. I felt like it was partially my fault. I've felt a lot of things, like if I wasn't misbehaving when I lived with my great-grandparents, I wouldn't have went to this man. Then, I blame myself because I was really bad and they had to tell the agency that they couldn't take care of me any more because I was being a problem. So I blame myself for that. If I was better when I was with my grandparents and didn't cause problems, this would have never happened to me. I would be with my great-grandparents. So I kind of blame myself again there, saying that it was my fault that this was going on.

INTERVIEWER: And how did if affect your thoughts about sex and sexuality?

JASON: I thought that it was okay to have sex with males. I started going out having sex with males and would use it to show love and affection. My dad took care of me and supplied things for me, so I felt that was his way of showing love and he really did love me. If he didn't love me anymore, he could always send me back to the agency. So I felt he wanted to take care of me and give me a family. I just felt I was okay. I started experimenting with other people older than me, some people younger than me.

INTERVIEWER: And how old were you when you first offended?

JASON: When I first offended, I was fifteen.

INTERVIEWER: And how old were your victims?

JASON: My first victim, she was eleven.

INTERVIEWER: And how do you know or have you worked on how your being victimized played a part in your offenses?

JASON: Yeah. There is a lot of similarities. Asking the sexual questions, as my father did to me. Picking younger people that are more vulnerable and more easier to convince.

INTERVIEWER: And how do you think that your being sexually victimized affects you today, if it affects you today?

JASON: It affects me today. It affects me a whole lot because the early sexual encounters really played a big part in me being a victimizer and having the sexual fantasies and the thoughts because it showed me a new light to another world. Being victimized, it showed me that some things were okay and doing this to other people is okay because it was done to me. I felt like if it was done to me, it must be okay because I didn't think my dad would do anything to hurt me.

INTERVIEWER: So you still struggle with knowing what's okay and what's not okay?

JASON: Yeah. Good relationships and bad relationships, boundaries, having conversations with people. When I am talking to people, like peers, somehow I always turn the conversation into a sexual conversation. It is very difficult to keep myself from not doing that, because it gave me high urges. After it was done to me, I just kept going out and just doing it with everybody and experimenting a whole bunch. It became addictive, like turning it from something I wanted, to something I felt that I needed. When I felt down and bad, or something happened that got me upset, I used this to fulfill the hurt and the pain to make me feel better about myself or the situation. Like I said, I felt loved when I was doing this and this is the way I show love to people and the way I got love for myself.

INTERVIEWER: Are there other ways that you are affected now? Anything else that you struggle with now?

JASON: I struggle with relationship building – building a relationship with people that is non-sexual. Being around older males makes me very uncomfortable. Expressing myself and my true feelings to people. If I am feeling down or upset about something, it is hard to go to someone and open up to somebody. It has been really hard for me to stay on key and on track in my treatment. Those urges are just so overwhelming sometimes, it is very hard for me to control them. I have to admit sometimes I fall back in my treatment, or when I have these high urges, I don't let someone know... I keep it inside. I don't tell anybody and then I wind up relapsing and falling back in treatment.

INTERVIEWER: Anything else? Do you ever have any nightmares or flashbacks, or anything like that?

JASON: I've had some nightmares where the abusing would replay in my dream. That would trigger me into depression and you know, want me to feel loved again. Then I wind up acting out because I was so depressed I wanted to feel happy again and loved, and feel good about myself. That is the only real way that I knew how to get love from other people. I was never taught that just being able to sit down and talk to someone can be just as loving as having sex.

INTERVIEWER: Anything else you want to say?

JASON: No.

Questions about Jason Victim # 1

1. How were this young man's beliefs about trust affected by his sexual abuse? __________

____

____

____

____

____

2. How did his victimization effect his beliefs about sexuality? ______________________

____

____

____

____

____

3. In what ways does sexual abuse at an early age have a negative effect on the sexual identity of a male? ____

____

____

____

____

4. How does this person's victimization play a part in his own sexual abusing? ________

5. Which of this young man's beliefs need to change to prevent him from re-abusing? ___

6. If you put yourself in Jason's place, what would you do (specifically) to change your belief system in order to keep from re-abusing? ________________

Interview With Chris Victim of Sexual Abuse #2

This is an interview with a second male victim of sexual abuse. Read Chris's story, while trying to empathize with his feelings. Then answer the questions at the end of the interview.

INTERVIEWER: How old were you when you were first sexually victimized?

CHRIS: I was three years old.

INTERVIEWER: And who sexually victimized you?

CHRIS: Well, my aunt.

INTERVIEWER: And can you say what happened?

CHRIS: Well, I don't remember much, but what I do remember is she was babysitting me and my mom was going somewhere and all I can remember is we went into a bathtub. She gave us a bath and she made us do something. I don't know what it was.

INTERVIEWER: And then, were you sexually victimized again?

CHRIS: Well, yes.

INTERVIEWER: And how old were you then?

CHRIS: I was about six or seven at the time.

INTERVIEWER: Can you talk a little bit about what happened then?

CHRIS: Well, I was raped by my stepfather at the time. It was my birthday. He took me into the bathroom. I was having fun and I had to use the bathroom, so I asked my mom. He said he would volunteer, so he took me. I went in first and used the bathroom. He came in following me and he told me to stand up on the toilet and I did. He stripped me of all my clothes and he anally penetrated me and made me perform oral sex on him.

INTERVIEWER: Did he do that once or more than one time?

CHRIS: More than once.

INTERVIEWER: And it started when you were how old?

CHRIS: About six or seven.

INTERVIEWER: And when did that continue until?

CHRIS: I was eight, but also during that time I was abused by another man who was a friend of my stepfather. I was outside playing tag once, no, it was hide-and-go-seek in the neighborhood. I came in because I was tired and thirsty. He was obviously drunk; you could tell. He anally raped me.

INTERVIEWER: Did that happen once, or more than once?

CHRIS: Just that one incident, but he abused me more than that.

INTERVIEWER: Sexually?

CHRIS: Yes.

INTERVIEWER: And then, did anyone else sexually abuse you?

CHRIS: My brother.

INTERVIEWER: And how old were you when that happened?

CHRIS: Eleven or twelve.

INTERVIEWER: And how old was your brother?

CHRIS: About fifteen or sixteen.

INTERVIEWER: Can you talk about that?

CHRIS: It was in my room. Actually, I had come back from playing basketball with some friends and went upstairs. First, I went into my room, wrapped a towel around my waist, and went to the bathroom and took my shower. He was standing in my room when I came back. I cursed at him and he said, "Don't you threaten me," and he pulled out a knife and took the towel from around my waste. He performed oral sex on me and then he anally penetrated me.

INTERVIEWER: Can you talk about the way that would happen to you and how you were victimized has an impact on you now?

CHRIS: I have a hard time talking to people. It is hard for me to be around men or adults. I have that, "I don't trust attitude" towards people. It is hard for me to go into places and be an adult sometimes.

INTERVIEWER: Does it affect you in any other ways?

CHRIS: I question my own sexuality sometimes. Because I was abused by both male and female. And sometimes I question my own sexuality.

INTERVIEWER: What is that like for you?

CHRIS: It is difficult because I know how homosexuals are treated in this world and it is not pretty. It is really not pretty.

INTERVIEWER: Do you feel like the fact that you were sexually abused impacted on your sexual practices?

CHRIS: You mean my offenses?

INTERVIEWER: Your sexual preferences.

CHRIS: Sometimes, normal. Sometimes I just don't let them bother me. I think I choose female over male any day of the week.

INTERVIEWER: But sometimes it can be confusing?

CHRIS: Yeah... sometimes. When I sit down I think about it sometimes. It confuses me, not a heck of a lot, but sometimes.

INTERVIEWER: What are some other ways that you have been affected by it? Has it affected your life?

CHRIS: Well, I have been in programs for most of my life. I've been in programs for 11 years and you know the world is out there changing and I'm still the same. Sometimes I think like a kid, you know, I get happy, or too excited, and act like a kid sometimes.

INTERVIEWER: What about your offenses? How do you think being victimized has impacted you in terms of your offenses?

CHRIS: Well, maybe I felt powerless when I was being victimized, so I victimized my three sisters in order to get that power. Or to get revenge on people, so I took it out on someone else instead of dealing with that person, or I should say people.

INTERVIEWER: What about any feelings or difficulty expressing feelings or monitoring your feelings?

CHRIS: It doesn't affect me a lot. I have a hard time expressing my feelings out loud, but if you give me a piece of paper and a pen, I can express my feelings. I put it into poems and that's how I tell people and tell the world what is going on inside me and how I am feeling. I'm not a people person... I like being by myself.

INTERVIEWER: Do you think that your being victimized played any role in that?

CHRIS: Yeah... I think so. You know having that lack of trust in people. So, I tend to be by myself.

INTERVIEWER: When you say that you don't trust people, is it a fear that people will hurt you?

CHRIS: Yeah, I think so.

INTERVIEWER: What are some of the day to day things that you have to deal with as a result of being victimized?

CHRIS: I have to deal with flashbacks, bad dreams, and nightmares.

INTERVIEWER: What are the dreams, nightmares and flashbacks like?

CHRIS: Pure hell.

INTERVIEWER: And they relate to your being offended?

CHRIS: It's like third person, a ghost or a shadow. I just see it happen and I can't do nothing about it.

INTERVIEWER: Does what you are experiencing now, the flashbacks, the nightmares, the dreams, and the difficulties you experienced because of being sexually offended, does that scare you for the future?

CHRIS: Yeah.

INTERVIEWER: Can you talk a little bit about that?

CHRIS: It makes me think about, do I have a future? It makes me wonder if I have a future. Am I going to, you know, relapse. I question myself... I'm scared too. I really don't want to because I've got dreams and I know if I go to jail I can never achieve my goals. I don't want to grow up and if I have a kid I don't want him growing up and people say, "Oh, where is your daddy"? And he has to say, "He's in jail." I don't want people to say that about me.

Questions about Chris Victim # 2

1. How did Chris's sexual abuse affect his beliefs about himself? ____________________

____

____

____

____

2. How did the multiple victimization affect Chris's beliefs about trust? ________________

____

____

____

____

3. If you were Chris, what beliefs would you change about yourself so you would not re-offend? ____

____

____

____

____

____

4. If you were Chris, what would you do in order build trust in others? ________________

____

____

____

____

____

5. Pretend you were one of the perpetrators that sexually abused Chris and write an apology letter to him. ______

6. Respond to your letter now, as if you were Chris. Tell the abuser what kind of a person you would be today if he had not abused you (e.g., your belief system). ______

Interview With Nick Victim of Emotional Abuse #3

INTERVIEWER: What's the worst thing that has happened to you?

NICK: My parents splitting up and then my grandmother's verbal abuse.

INTERVIEWER: When is your first memory of your grandmother being verbally abusive?

NICK: When me and my brother were like 3 and 5 years old.

INTERVIEWER: How did you know it was abusive?

NICK: Basically because she had us tied to a chair.

INTERVIEWER: Why did she tie you two to the chair?

NICK: Me and my brother were running around the house and she didn't want to deal with us so she tied us up to some chairs.

INTERVIEWER: So you and your brother where just running around doing regular kid stuff?

NICK: Yes.

INTERVIEWER: How long did she tie you two up?

NICK: Three to four hours.

INTERVIEWER: How did she tie you two up? I mean could you two talk to each other?

NICK: She tied our hands to each side of the chairs with my right hand tied to his left and my left hand to his right hand and she tied our legs to the chairs.

INTERVIEWER: What did you say to each other? Did you cry?

NICK: No.

INTERVIEWER: Why didn't you say anything? You had to think this was crazy?

NICK: Because I was scared. Yeah, I thought it was crazy, somewhat.

INTERVIEWER: What other types of abuse did she demonstrate?

NICK: Telling me I wasn't a part of the family and I didn't belong.

INTERVIEWER: Why would she say that?

NICK: Because I'm adopted.

INTERVIEWER: Didn't she say that to your brother too because he's adopted, right?

NICK: Not when I was around.

INTERVIEWER: What was her problem?

NICK: I have no idea.

INTERVIEWER: What else about her behavior was crazy, weird, or abusive?

NICK: No, nothing else.

INTERVIEWER: How long did her abusive behavior last?

NICK: Thirteen years and still going.

INTERVIEWER: How detrimental has this abuse been to you?

NICK: (unresponsive).

INTERVIEWER: On a scale of 1-10, with 10 being the most detrimental, how would you rate her abusive behaviors to you?

NICK: Ten.

INTERVIEWER: How has this abuse been detrimental to you?

NICK: I don't really try to get close to anyone. I'll talk to anyone but I won't really trust them.

INTERVIEWER: How do you avoid getting close to people?

NICK: I won't tell them any personal stuff.

INTERVIEWER: Do you lie more because of the abusive behavior or try to hide or mask your true self?

NICK: A little bit.

INTERVIEWER: Do you feel damaged because of this abuse? Will you recover?

NICK: Yeah. Eventually now that I'm not living with her and I don't have to see her.

INTERVIEWER: How is the impact of her abuse different from other forms of abuse?

NICK: It was all basically the same. No more. No less.

INTERVIEWER: How does it compare to your past history of contracting genital warts from a sexual partner?

NICK: It was basically all the same.

INTERVIEWER: When did you begin to display behavioral problems?

NICK: Since the fourth grade (eight years ago).

INTERVIEWER: Are you able to have an intimate relationship?

NICK: I won't tell them any personal stuff.

INTERVIEWER: Do you exhibit any abusive behaviors now?

NICK: Yes.

INTERVIEWER: Was your acting out behavior due to you not feeling good about yourself?

NICK: Yes, a little. Maybe 50%. Yes.

INTERVIEWER: Describe your acting out behaviors.

NICK: Smoking, drinking, getting kicked out of schools, being bisexual.

INTERVIEWER: How would you be different if you were not verbally and emotionally abused by your grandmother?

NICK: I probably wouldn't have started smoking and everything else and I wouldn't be here now.

Questions about Nick Victim # 3

1. What trust beliefs were violated for Nick?______________________________

2. How did the abuse by his grandmother change his views of the world?____________

3. How did his beliefs about empathy change by being tied to the chair? ____________

4. How would his beliefs about his grandmother affect his beliefs about males?________

5. If you were Nick, how would this abuse affect your thoughts?__________________

Interview With Roger Victim of Physical Abuse #4

INTERVIEWER: Briefly describe each member of your family. Please indicate who resides with you and include their names and ages.

ROGER: Heather, 15 – she's getting into trouble lately. She got into a fight with a girl and beat her up and she got locked up while I was locked up for getting into a fight. We were locked up at the same place at the same time actually. Adam and Brandon, 7 – they look up to me a lot. They are bad.

INTERVIEWER: Bad like what?

ROGER: They do all bad things and they don't listen at all. They curse and fight each other and are disrespectful.

ROGER: Mom, 30's – she's like every other mom, I guess.

INTERVIEWER: Are you closer to your mom than your dad?

ROGER: Yeah.

INTERVIEWER: What does your mom do?

ROGER: Meals on wheels.

ROGER: Dad – he is in his early 30's, I guess. He does floor coverings, installs carpets. We haven't really talked much until a couple of weeks before I got locked up. My dad, I don't know how old he is either. I don't really know much about him at all.

INTERVIEWER: How can you live in somebody's house in the same house and be blood (not like crypt or the gang blood) but be in the same house and not talk? I mean I would rather someone be in my face yell and curse me out.

ROGER: That is the only time we did talk. We would curse and all that stuff. We did it a lot and I didn't like it, so I tried to avoid it and that is just by avoiding him and he did the same. We did it… I guess we were pretty stubborn but we did it for about seventeen years.

INTERVIEWER: He may be stubborn. You might be smart. What are some of your first memories of your dad?

ROGER: My first memories from the beginning when I was born. Actually I think how some dads are in jail and prison when their kids are born. Mine was in a detention center. My dad was in "Juvee." He was only sixteen when he had me and my mom was only fourteen. So, he was either in it or just got out of a detention center. So he wasn't there when I was born. I don't really ever remember him ever when I was really really young. Like I thought my uncle was my dad. I used to call him dad. My first memories of my father were I think of him yelling at me for not finishing my food or something like that. We were living in a hotel. And going back to my other house where he lived and we walked in. The house that I lived in was the house I grew up in. Basically was a two bedroom house.

INTERVIEWER: With all those people in it?

ROGER: Yeah, now there's six of us in there.

INTERVIEWER: Six people in a two-bedroom?

ROGER: Yeah. I remember like walking in and there was this big crate and it was full with rubber wrestlers, like wrestling guys, and a TV on a crate.

INTERVIEWER: Wrestling guys?

ROGER: No, no, no, like they were like little toys and a TV right there. I hated going. I hated going there. Cause my dad was always like an asshole. I didn't like him.

INTERVIEWER: How was he an A-hole? I mean, because he would only argue, fuss, curse, what?

ROGER: Then like, I just remember he would just be angry. Angry, and like drunk, I guess.

INTERVIEWER: How would he show the anger? Would he throw things?

ROGER: I just remember his face looking mean. He would always be punching holes in the wall and he would be in my momma's face screaming and hollering.

INTERVIEWER: So you would see them fussing and fighting and him like actually punching holes in the wall? Or would you just walk in and you'd see the hole in the wall?

ROGER: Yeah, I'd see him punch holes in the wall.

INTERVIEWER: So, that had to scare you a little bit?

ROGER: Yeah, it used to. Then like my sister was born. We'd be laying asleep in our beds and like we would hear screaming and hollering like every night. Just screams. I'd always go out there and they'd be fighting and he would be drunk or high or whatever. I didn't know at the time. My mom would… like he'd come home late and my mom would be like, "Let me smell your breath." She's like, "You're fucking drinking again," and they'd be arguing and he'd be screaming. Me and my sister would be like in the doorway. We would be in our living room or in the kitchen where they are. My sister was screaming and I'd get like mad and angry. Sometimes I'd go after him or say something to him.

INTERVIEWER: Is this to protect your mom or –?

ROGER: Yeah, because my sister is screaming and my mom is crying and I'm just like I don't know what to do. I hate that guy anyway. I hate him cause every time when he's around someone gets upset.

INTERVIEWER: Even now?

ROGER: No.

INTERVIEWER: Do you ever have good memories of your parents?

ROGER: (Long hesitation). No.

INTERVIEWER: Did you ever see your parents get along?

ROGER: Yeah! I mean they don't do it. They never went out or did anything. They never like really talked. They never did anything.

INTERVIEWER: Did you ever see them look like a couple? Like hugging and kissing or playing around like you would with your girlfriend?

ROGER: Um, no. Once in a while. But not really.

INTERVIEWER: Did you ever see your parents kiss or…?

ROGER: Kiss in the morning on the way to work.

INTERVIEWER: Did they ever say that they even loved each other?

ROGER: Once in a while.

INTERVIEWER: What was the craziest thing you remember about your family?

ROGER: When I was really, really young, my mom threw me and my sister in the car. She was driving away. My dad was in back of 'em, chasing us in the car. We came to a stop sign and he jumped out of the other car and started choking my mom. And ah, it is the first time I think I ever said a bad word. "Get your fucking…" I said, "something fucking" and screamed it really loud. Then she stepped on the gas I think or he let her go maybe. Then we wrecked. I don't know, but I didn't say nothing then while he was doing it. Then I stuck my head out of the window and I said something to him. Like he was walking back and I said, "Just let her go." Somehow, I think he stopped again. He said, "Don't you ever say something like that again."

INTERVIEWER: What interrupted him from choking your mom? Was it her pushing down on the accelerator?

ROGER: Nah, I don't remember. Then, at my grandmother's house, he was choking her again. They were fighting, arguing. My uncle was doing something to her, like holding her. It is really hard to remember because I was really young. I remember I was scared.

INTERVIEWER: When you say "your uncle," do you mean your mom's brother?

ROGER: Yeah.

INTERVIEWER: So, your uncle and your mom were fighting?

ROGER: He was holding her arms behind her back. I looked up to him, but he let me down. I remember there was someone else I looked up to, and I told him that. He said, "Don't ever look up to somebody because they always fucking let you down." So, now I try to be my own person. I looked up to another person and that was my cousin, Jamie. He put me in the hospital one time. He was drunk and he was choking his girlfriend. He was a really, really, really big guy. Like cause he used to use steroids. He's like humongous. He had a party at his house and he got really drunk and he started choking his girlfriend. Nobody did anything, so I pushed him off her and said, "What are you doing?" I turned around and he clocked me. I slid and hit my head on the wall. The doctor said it could have been really serious if he had hit me any harder because it was near my temple. I had a sprained neck, a concussion, my lip got split.

INTERVIEWER: It sounds like the majority of fights you have been in have occurred when you tried to stand up for someone else and it is the main reason why you are here?

ROGER: Yeah, both of my aggravated assault charges occurred when two different kids were getting picked on.

INTERVIEWER: So, what are some other things your dad used to do to you?

ROGER: He used to hit me a lot. He wouldn't have a reason, but he'd always say, "Don't give me a reason to hit you." I didn't understand it. I wouldn't give him a reason to hit me, but he'd do it anyway.

INTERVIEWER: He choked your mom. Did he ever choke you?

ROGER: Yeah.

INTERVIEWER: Did he choke you to the point you were unconscious?

ROGER: No.

INTERVIEWER: What all would he hit you with? Hands, chair?

ROGER: His hands mostly. Belts.

INTERVIEWER: Electric cords?

ROGER: Yeah, I've been hit with those before.

INTERVIEWER: Did you ever get to a point where you were no longer afraid of him?

ROGER: Yeah, I remember him beating the piss out of me, and I just remember standing there, trying to be like tough as hell. So he started to walk out and I said, "That didn't do nothing." Then he'd come back and beat my ass again.

INTERVIEWER: Did you ever try to sneak him?

ROGER: Um, no. He's faster than me. I remember one time, I don't remember what I did, but I remember like he picked up like a bat, and I don't remember whether it was a plastic bat or a wooden bat, but he chased me around the house. Two or three laps around the house. My house is big anyway, but he came running and caught me and beat my ass.

INTERVIEWER: Outside? The neighbors didn't see him?

ROGER: Nobody was around.

INTERVIEWER: Yeah, that's right you live?

ROGER: He never hit my siblings. That would make me mad too.

INTERVIEWER: So he beat you the most?

ROGER: I was the only one. I didn't understand it.

ROGER: I remember one time, it was near Christmas and there was this couch that he was sitting in, and I don't know why I did it, but I went over and sat in his lap and he pushed me off. Then, my sister came into the room and she sat on his lap and he didn't do anything about it to her.

INTERVIEWER: Why did he do that?

ROGER: I don't know why he did that! I was like what the hell is this about?

INTERVIEWER: Would it help you to know why he did that? Would it make a difference to you? There is only an obvious reason and I don't know it all.

ROGER: What's that?

INTERVIEWER: Picture this. He was sixteen when he had you. What do most sixteen year olds like to do?

ROGER: They like to party.

INTERVIEWER: And like you at sixteen, he too must have wanted to have sex and party. I mean I'm just calling a spade a spade. I mean I'm not trying to harp on that but, I think he knew he had to take on his responsibility. It was something he chose to do but I think he hated the fact that at sixteen he could not be a party animal. So I think for him, I mean I am not trying to make you feel bad, but I think you may need to know why he treated you differently. But sometimes, the why can matter. But I would imagine it was a time that he realized, almost at the start of his social and sexual development, the time when people are generally their wildest, that he could no longer party and he had to be a responsible adult. He had to step up. And at sixteen, I think he hated that. He could not be a party animal. He could not have a sexual or social freedom as a teenager or as a young adult anymore. He prematurely was forced to grow up and he resented that in you and himself. Don't let that haunt or harm you.

ROGER: I'm over it now.

INTERVIEWER: It is easier for him to go off on you. Sometimes you can't go off on yourself. It is easier at least for someone to go off on someone else. You can't truly avoid yourself.

Questions about Roger Victim #4

1. How did the exposure to his dad's violence affect his beliefs about himself? __________

____

____

____

____

2. How did his dad's violence affect his beliefs about trust? __________

____

____

____

____

3. If you were Roger, how would you try to change your beliefs about men? __________

____

____

____

____

4. Pretend you were Roger's dad and write a letter of apology to him. __________

____

____

____

____

5. If you were Roger, what would you do to develop healthy relationships with females?

____

____

____

____

Interview With Mike Victim of Bullying #5

INTERVIEWER: As I told you earlier, this is an interview about your history of being bullied. When did the bullying start?

MIKE: You could say like when I was in the second grade or third grade. I just started being quiet. I wasn't saying nothing to nobody. I guess everybody thought that "He is the quiet kid in the classroom. We can bully him." People would just pick on me, throwing stuff at me.

INTERVIEWER: What does it mean for you to be bullied? What does that mean? Because I'm sure like different people played like the "dirty dozens" and stuff like that. You know, like the "Your mama" jokes – that may or may not be bullying. What do you think bullying is for you?

MIKE: Being the littlest kid in the class, or for some people it was the fattest kid in the class. When you are quiet, some people just pick on you, throwing stuff at you, and talk about your mama, and doing stuff like that.

INTERVIEWER: So it's being a target?

MIKE: Yeah.

INTERVIEWER: Like somebody talking about you and stuff like that? What about like getting beaten up? Is that the same thing or is there a difference?

MIKE: Yeah.

INTERVIEWER: So getting picked on or joked on is the same as getting beaten up?

MIKE: Yeah.

INTERVIEWER: Even though it's different, right?

MIKE: Yeah.

INTERVIEWER: You get hurt a different way, right? One is physical and the other is emotional.

MIKE: Yeah.

INTERVIEWER: So you said in second grade you got kind of quiet and because you were kind of quiet people saw you as being shy. They started picking on you?

MIKE: Yeah.

INTERVIEWER: Was it everybody or like one or two main people?

MIKE: Like one person would say something and the whole class would just like join in.

INTERVIEWER: What are some of the things they would say?

MIKE: They would say something about my mom or I'm dirty.

INTERVIEWER: They would say something like you're dirty?

MIKE: Yeah.

INTERVIEWER: Not trying to be funny, but I mean were you dirty or would they just make up stuff like…?

MIKE: I wasn't dirty. It was just like I didn't have like what everybody else had. I didn't have like name brand stuff.

INTERVIEWER: Okay.

MIKE: I didn't have like Nike or Jordans. I didn't have all of that. I just had what my mom could afford for us, not what we wanted, but what we needed. Like they would say, "He's got on dirty sneakers, so we can pick on him," and stuff like that.

INTERVIEWER: Okay.

MIKE: Basically.

INTERVIEWER: So how did you… would you cry about it or what?

MIKE: I would get mad and go home and tell my mom about it. She used to tell me "Miserable people, they just need company." She'd tell me and I would just go on with the day. Sometimes I'd cry. As I got older I started getting picked on and bullied because I went to a foster home. They would like pick on me 'cause I was in a foster home. I couldn't take it no more. People just kept picking on me. So I started picking back on people. So when I got bullied and someone new came to class, I started messing with them to get the attention off of me and put it on them. When I think about it, when I was getting bullied, I didn't like it. So why should I pick on this person?

INTERVIEWER: But you started doing it anyway?

MIKE: Yeah.

INTERVIEWER: Just so you wouldn't…

MIKE: Get picked on.

INTERVIEWER: Are there any things that people would say? You said "dirty" and some other stuff, but like you said people picked on people if they were quiet, if they were fat. Is there anything else they said other than "dirty" or was it just "dirty"?

MIKE: Basically just "dirty." That's what it really was, "dirty."

INTERVIEWER: You said they picked on your mom. They would tease you.

MIKE: "Your mom is this," and "Your mom is fat," and like everybody had "your mom" jokes.

INTERVIEWER: Right, but were they accurate jokes or were they somewhat accurate jokes?

MIKE: Some were accurate and some weren't.

INTERVIEWER: Okay. And the stuff that made you cry, was that some stuff that you believed, or something you could not change?

MIKE: Yeah.

INTERVIEWER: So how long would you say you were being bullied before you actually flipped the script and you started bullying other people?

MIKE: When I got in the fifth grade. I started picking on other people so I could stop being picked on.

INTERVIEWER: So, from second to fifth grade. After about three years, you started picking on other people just so you would not get the spotlight?

MIKE: Yeah.

INTERVIEWER: Did you ever see anybody or make anybody cry to your knowledge?

MIKE: No.

INTERVIEWER: But you were joking then pretty hard though, right?

MIKE: (He smiles).

INTERVIEWER: You already started smiling, dude.

MIKE: They didn't ever cry. From what I'd seen, they didn't ever cry.

INTERVIEWER: But you tried to go for them and really get them right?

MIKE: Yeah.

INTERVIEWER: So you were pretty good at playing the "dozens" and talking about "your mama" and stuff like that?

MIKE: Yeah. Some people would say stuff like, "Your mom is on welfare," this that and the third. But it be the same people that say, "My mama's on welfare" that night or the night before that they was over my house eating or something. So, I'd get them right back with the saying, "My mom is this and my mom is that, but you was over my house eating such and such a night." Some people would say something about my mom, but they never even seen my mom. And I basically knew everybody's mom in the class though. If I had jokes, it was all real.

INTERVIEWER: Why did you get to see everybody's mom and they couldn't see yours?

MIKE: It's like when I was being bad in school, my mom didn't come up to the school much. She would come up once in a while, but she wouldn't come to school much unless she was coming to pick us up.

INTERVIEWER: But you got to meet everybody else's mom? How's that?

MIKE: 'Cause like my mom, like when we had to go on field trips, like my mom she had to work, or she was like pregnant with my brother at the time and could not make it to the field trip. So like mostly everybody's mom could make it for the field trips and whatever. Like I remember this one boy, I was like picking on him, and I was picking on him through his whole third grade class and whatever, but when we had a field trip my mom couldn't make it 'cause she was pregnant with my little brother. So, I went with his mom on the field trip. That made me feel like some kind of way. I'm like picking on this boy, but his mom, she drove me in her car on the field trip. So, he and I became good friends.

INTERVIEWER: Okay. Do you ever remember being beaten up, like jumped, kicked, or would people trip you in the halls or throw paper at you and stuff like that?

MIKE: When we were at school on the bus, people would throw spitballs at me. There was this one boy, he was just bigger than me. So I was scared of him. Everyday he'd like mess with me. I'd get on the bus and he'd like throw something at me. He would throw spitballs at me. One day I was coming up the hall and he tripped me and my nose started bleeding. And one day like he beat me up a couple of times. He jumped me before.

INTERVIEWER: For no reason?

MIKE: Yeah. Just for no reason. He just didn't like me. I don't know if it was something I said to him, but he just beat me up. He just picked on me like everyday. Everyday.

INTERVIEWER: Did you ever say something to him like "Stop" or "Leave me alone"?

MIKE: I told the teacher on him. That didn't do nothing to him, but it made it worse. He just bothered me more.

INTERVIEWER: So the teacher didn't like follow up?

MIKE: No. His mom came to the school a couple of times and he got suspended, but when he came back to school he'd still bother me. So I just stopped telling the teacher. I'd tell on him and he would get suspended, but he would come back and I would get it ten times worse.

INTERVIEWER: Did you ever try to get revenge on him, or sneak up on him or something like that, or get somebody else to beat him up?

MIKE: Yeah.

INTERVIEWER: Yeah, you did? Why you didn't tell me about that? What's that about?

MIKE: One day we had pizza and I was with him and my mom. We had to wear uniforms to school and we couldn't get our clothes dirty 'cause we really didn't have a lot of clothes back then. And I was wearing a white buttoned-down shirt and he ran into me on purpose and smacked pizza on me and got pizza all on my shirt. I knew I was going to get in trouble with my mom. After that, I don't know, it's funny that my little sister helped me out. My little sister, when she was young, acted like a tomboy. I didn't really fight that much after school. My sister seen me and what happened – and my sister punched him in his face. So, he didn't ever say nothing to me after that.

INTERVIEWER: You didn't even put her up to that, she did that on her on?

MIKE: Yeah. After school she seen him and he had taken my book bag, so my sister punched him in his face. I told the teacher on him 'cause he took my book bag.

INTERVIEWER: Did you ever get your book bag back?

MIKE: Yeah.

INTERVIEWER: Okay.

MIKE: He didn't ever say nothing to me no more. Now, my little sister calls on me to help her out.

INTERVIEWER: What's the worst thing you remember about being bullied? Have you already discussed it or what?

MIKE: Getting beaten up in front of the whole school.

INTERVIEWER: That wasn't that same dude?

MIKE: No. It was a different dude. He would mess with me every day. It wasn't like I was getting bullied 'cause I would mess with him back. One day he did something to me. He just kept throwing stuff at me and I kept letting it go. I didn't want to get into trouble. I just came back off of suspension. I didn't want to get into trouble. He hit me or something, and he hit me in the lunchroom, so we walked outside the lunchroom and started fighting. We had a good fight, but he beat me up though in front of the whole school. That was like the worst thing that ever happened to me when I got bullied – 'cause it was in front of a whole bunch of girls.

INTERVIEWER: Did anybody ever take your lunch money?

MIKE: I got my lunch money taken once or twice, that's about it.

INTERVIEWER: How did you end it?

MIKE: I told his mom so he got in trouble. So I stopped that.

INTERVIEWER: Is this the same guy?

MIKE: No.

INTERVIEWER: How many different people bullied you?

MIKE: Like four.

INTERVIEWER: Did they bully you about being in a foster home?

MIKE: Yeah. At times I would cry about it 'cause I wanted to be at home but I was in a foster home for about 6 months. And after awhile I couldn't do anything about it and crying about it didn't help, so I just ignored it.

INTERVIEWER: Do you bully anybody now?

MIKE: No.

Questions about Mike Victim #5

1. What did bullying do to affect Mike's trust in others?____________________

2. How do you think he felt when he was tripped in front of the whole school?

3. How did Mike feel when the bullies made fun of his mom? ____________________

4. What were Mike's beliefs about his own self-esteem when that happened? __________

5. How can he change his beliefs about himself now? ______________________________

6. What do you think the long term effects will be on Mike? ______________________________

7. Pretend you are the bully in this case and write an apology letter to Mike: ______________

Interview With Dominic Victim of Bullying #6

INTERVIEWER: Today we are going to talk about your history of being bullied. Give me the first experience you remember of being bullied.

DOMINIC: My first significant experience of being bullied occurred when I was at the bus stop waiting for the bus. This kid Sam is a year or two older than me and we got into an argument or something and he spit on me, on my jacket.

INTERVIEWER: Was he bigger than you? Because you're a big guy.

DOMINIC: Well, at the time he was.

INTERVIEWER: Was Sam only bullying you? Why was he focused on you?

DOMINIC: I can't remember why he was solely focused on me.

INTERVIEWER: Of the times you do remember being bullied, can you tell me why they focused on you? What were some of the things they would call you?

DOMINIC: They said all kinds of things about my name. I've heard this a million times – "{name of a breakfast cereal}."

INTERVIEWER: Do you think you minimize how much or how often you have been bullied? Both your mother and the documentation seems to suggest that you have been bullied a lot. But now you seem to have so little to share about these experiences?

DOMINIC: 'Cause I didn't take it so much as bullying. Certain instances, like the one I told you about, like that spitting one. Maybe one or two more I could say those (instances) were bullying. The rest I could say were just joking around. Another thing they would joke on me about was I was like really, really skinny. So they would joke on me about that.

INTERVIEWER: Did they call you a specific name? Come on, what is the worst thing bullies have done or said to you? What bothered you the most? If you could play a videotape back in your head now, what would the worst thing be? What would that picture look like?

DOMINIC: One thing my brother used to say about me being skinny was that I had to run around in the shower to get wet, or "Turn sideways 'cause we can't see you anymore."

INTERVIEWER: Do you think it is possible you have some distortions about being teased? Because to me the difference of being bullied versus being teased is that when you are being bullied, you are dealing with someone taking something from you that is significant. It sounds like there is a discrepancy between what you perceive as bullying and being teased.

Being teased and bullied can be the same thing but it has to do with the severity of the emotional affect on you. That's what is being taken from you when you are bullied, your dignity and self-respect. It is the inability to say, "Stop," "No," or "Don't." "Don't talk about me like that anymore!" It can affect people differently. You seem to shut down and internalize these negative instances. But you later tell yourself something different to compensate. But still something is taken away from you in order for you to need to compensate.

DOMINIC: There was one time on the bus where everybody started cracking on me, but I don't remember what they were saying. But after awhile it finally got to me and I started crying.

INTERVIEWER: Where did you go when you were crying? Did you go to your room?

DOMINIC: No, I was still on the bus. I didn't go anywhere.

INTERVIEWER: I think everyone falls short in some area that their peers pick on them or tease them about. Everybody experiences some type of verbal abuse or bullying.

DOMINIC: Yeah! How did they tease you?

INTERVIEWER: Well, if it will help you, then I have no problem self-disclosing. When I was growing up, kids would always play the "dirty dozens," where people would pick on each other saying something derogatory like, "You are so ugly" or "Your breath smells so funky that…" And then the other person would simply respond by saying, "Your mama…" At times even best friends would engage in playing the dirty dozens just to keep in practice. No one wanted to be humiliated in front of their peers like that, so you had to be on point. You had to practice. Well, for me, kids would for the most part leave me alone because of my size and because my mom worked at my middle school and she didn't play. No one messed with her. There was one thing that bothers me even until this day. They would say, "You're chest is so big you need a D-sized bra." I was always a little chubby and my chest would vacillate between very muscular to breast-like depending on my diet and exercise. One thing about the dozens, it was funny at times to all of us, but it also shaped the way we saw ourselves. The irony of it all was that my peers were right. My chest was a little bigger than it should have been. At times, if I were not working out or eating my behind off, my chest would look like breasts and that ain't cool… I think everybody's got something they feel or believe that they have to work on or avoid just to feel normal. It took me the longest time before I would take off my shirt in public. Come on, you must have had similar experiences.

DOMINIC: No. Not me. I'm kidding. Of course I have, but I tell myself something to compensate for what they say about me.

INTERVIEWER: I would like to hear what has been said to you because you may not know the affect it may have on you until later.

DOMINIC: There have been a couple of times that I remember that I was being picked on and I left the school bus and went home crying, but that only happened a couple of times. They said some pretty mean stuff, but I don't remember exactly what they said. I just remembered that I never wanted to feel like that again.

INTERVIEWER: It's odd that you would not remember what they said, but you vividly remember crying about it. What about now, how do your peers pick on you? How do the other residents tease you?

DOMINIC: They call me, "brain washed" because I know a lot of the psychological jargon used to treat this population of kids.

INTERVIEWER: You mean Psychobabble?

DOMINIC: I don't know. I guess. I learned a lot at my previous placement 'cause I was there for so long.

INTERVIEWER: That nickname doesn't seem to bother you too much though?

DOMINIC: No, I've been called a lot worse.

INTERVIEWER: Yeah, I would imagine, but you don't seemingly remember that much about it either. Is it possible that their comments have bothered you so much and maybe on at least some level, you have internalized it so much that you don't differentiate what they have said with your own beliefs?

DOMINIC: Yeah, I guess so.

INTERVIEWER: You guess or you know?

DOMINIC: I guess but I'm not sure.

Questions for Dominic Victim #6:

1. In what ways does this victim of bullying minimize the pain of being bullied?

2. Do you think Dominic can deal with his scars from being bullied? If so, how?

3. Why do you think Dominic minimizes the pain of being bullied? Why do you think that he called it "being teased" rather than "being bullied"?

4. How do you think it felt for Dominic to cry on the bus in front of his peers?

5. How do you think the bullying effected Dominic's beliefs about his self worth?______

____

____

____

____

____

6. Write a letter to Dominic as if you were the bully. Try to see if you can get the victim to admit how badly it hurt and how he might fix it. ______________________

____

____

____

____

____

____

____

____

____

____

____

____

____

____

____

____

____

____

____

Questions About All of the Victims

What would you tell each of these victims to help them deal with their beliefs about themselves?

Jason Victim #1: ______________________________

____

____

____

____

____

Chris Victim #2: ______________________________

____

____

____

____

____

Nick Victim #3: ______________________________

____

____

____

____

____

Roger Victim #4: ______________________________

____

____

____

____

____

Mike Victim #5: ______________________________

____

____

____

____

____

Dominic Victim #6: ______________________________

____

____

____

____

____

10. Write five unhealthy beliefs that the victims have about abuse and five healthy beliefs.

Unhealthy Negative Beliefs	Rational Healthy Beliefs
(1)__________	(1)__________
(2)__________	(2)__________
(3)__________	(3)__________
(4)__________	(4)__________
(5)__________	(5)__________

CHAPTER 11
VICTIM TO VICTIMIZER TO SURVIVOR

Introduction

Congratulations! You have just completed the empathy chapter of the workbook. Some of the readings may have been very emotional for you. If painful emotions and disturbing thoughts popped into your head, it could be that you are re-experiencing parts of your own victimization.

Many abusers have been victims of sexual, physical, and/or emotional abuse. You may not want to disclose that you have been a victim. You may feel too embarrassed, scared, confused, or angry to talk about something that is very personal and painful.

Even though it is difficult to do, it is important to talk about victimization. Deep emotional pain cannot be stuffed away and forgotten. It will re-appear in other ways, especially as negative and aggressive behavior. Mental health professionals call this, "acting-out." The victim "acts-out" the pain that he or she cannot deal with by acting rude, nasty, violent, or sexually abusive.

Take a look at yourself and your life. Have you "acted-out" the pain of your victimization – by yelling, fighting, abusing or other behaviors – instead of dealing with it? Begin to pay closer attention to your feelings and thoughts when you are fearful, depressed, confused, or upset. You may have noticed that you have increased sexual urges, masturbation, drug abuse, or anger when you are feeling badly. The painful feelings that remain from your own victimization may be leading you to "act-out" in negative ways.

Some victims of physical and sexual abuse try not to feel anything. They "shut down" emotions and "numb" themselves as a way of handling emotional pain. But when people try to shut down painful emotions, they must also shut down positive emotions – and it can cause depression and anxiety. These feelings of depression and anxiety are often risk factors for abusive behavior.

This chapter is designed as a safe place to begin to examine your own victimization. It may help you to address how it plays a role in your own abusive behavior.

You cannot say for sure that you would not have become an abuser if you had not been a victim. You don't know where you would have gone, or what you could have become. If you are honest with yourself, work hard, and continue to work on your victim issues, you have the opportunity to become a survivor, not a victimizer.

Belief Analysis of My Victimization

Listed below are some common beliefs about being a victim. Please read each statement and rate how much you agree or disagree with each one.

1	2	3	4	5	6	7
Totally Disagree	Disagree Very Much	Disagree Slightly	Neutral	Agree Slightly	Agree Very Much	Totally Agree

____ 1. Being a victim of abuse has not changed me.

____ 2. I do not need to tell every detail of my victimization.

____ 3. It was partly my fault that I was abused.

____ 4. If I tell my story of abuse, my problems will be over.

____ 5. If I don't think about my abuse, it will go away.

____ 6. Why talk about the abuse, I will only feel bad.

____ 7. Sometimes I get real angry so that I don't feel the pain.

____ 8. I have problems trusting anyone.

____ 9. I didn't want to tell anyone about the abuse I suffered. I kept it secret.

____ 10. If someone gets too close to me, I do something to push them away.

____ 11. I am careful not to put myself into situations that may frighten me.

____ 12. Since my abuse, I often feel vulnerable.

____ 13. I am afraid I will become like my abuser.

____ 14. Whenever I feel helpless or not in control, I "act-out" to gain control.

____ 15. I feel like I need to be punished for being a victim.

____ 16. Since I was hurt (abused), it doesn't bother me to hurt (abuse) someone else.

____ 17. When I wanted to talk with someone about my victimization, no one would listen to me.

____ 18. I sometimes have thoughts about my victimization that I cannot control.

____ 19. If you were a victim, you will most likely become an abuser.

____ 20. If someone causes you pain, it's natural to want to inflict pain on someone else.

____ 21. I was abused and I turned out OK, so I probably didn't hurt my victim very much.

Common Thoughts and Feelings of Sexually Abused Children

As you explore your thoughts and feelings about your own victimization, it may be helpful to review the kinds of problems that are often experienced by child victims of sexual abuse, including:

- Guilt and shame.
- Nightmares.
- Anxiety and depression (sometimes including thoughts about suicide).
- Poor self-esteem and lack of self-confidence.
- Self-doubt in judgment about people and situations.
- Distrust and lack of trust in other people.
- Confusion about the proper behavior of adults and authority figures.
- Confusion about what a man should be and what a woman should be.
- Poor social relationships.

Victims of child sexual molestation may learn to relate to others sexually to get attention and may act out sexually at an early age. Some become sex abusers or prostitutes later in life. Many abuse drugs and/or alcohol.

Strong feelings of fear, rage, terror, loss of innocence, worthlessness, betrayal and isolation can cause an overwhelming sense of powerlessness and hopelessness for child victims of sexual abuse.

Child victims often blame themselves for the sexual abuse and see themselves as "damaged goods" or "dirty" or "bad." Victims of child sexual abuse feel "dirty" – as if they can never get clean again. Child victims feel like they are marked with a sign that tells other people, "Here I am – come and molest me, too."

Childhood victims are afraid to reveal their bodies to others (such as the shower in gym class or at the doctor's office) out of fear that someone will take advantage of them or find out that they have been sexually molested.

Some victims of child sexual abuse never feel normal. They might feel "different" from others. They often feel terribly alone or empty inside.

Questions To Help Yourself With Understanding Your Own Victimization

1. How old were you when you were first ______________________________? __________
(abuse committed against you)

2. Who ______________________________ you? ______________________________
(abuse committed against you) (abuser's name and relationship to you)

3. What was it like being with __________________ before you were __________________?
(abuser's name) (abuse)

____

____

4. Did __________________ treat you differently after the ______________________ began?
(abuser's name) (abuse)

How so? ____

____

5. Tell about the very first time you were ______________. What did __________________
(abuse) (abuser's name)
say to you? How did he/she first make you feel uncomfortable?

____

____

6. Where and when did the abuse happen to you? ______________________________

____

____

7. After the first time, did he/she keep abusing you in the same way, or did it change?

____

____

How did it change? ____

____

8. How often did ______________ _________________ you? _______________________
(abuser's name) (abuse) (once, daily, every week, etc.)

For how long were you abused? ____
(once, a few months, a year, many years, longer)

9. Where was everyone else in the family while this was happening? _________________

____

10. Did anyone else see you being _____________________ or know about it? If so, who?
(abuse)

____

11. Did _______________________ do this to anyone else you know?_________________
(abuser's name)

If yes, did you know about the other person(s) being ____________? ______________
(abuse)

____

____

12. How do you feel now about telling about what happened then? __________________

____

____

13. What did _________ tell you would happen if you told about being ______________?
(abuser) (abuse)

____

____

14. Describe how it felt to keep this secret. Did you want to tell someone? Who?

____

____

15. Did you try to tell someone? How?____

____

16. How old were you when people found out you were being ________________? ____
(abuse)

How did your parents find out this was happening to you? How did they react?

____

____

How did you feel after people discovered you were being abused?________________

____

____

____

Did your parents believe you? If not, did this change? ________________________

____

____

____

17. What happened after people found out? Who talked with you about it?__________

____

____

____

18. What happened to the person who abused you? Did you have to leave your home?

____

____

19. Did ________________ admit to the ________________ or deny it? ____________
(abuser's name) (abuse against you)

What did he/she say about the abuse committed against you? What cognitive distortions did he/she use? Did he/she make excuses? Minimize the seriousness of the abuse? Blame you?

____

____

20. How did your victimization change you as a person? How did it change your beliefs about yourself? About sex? About people? ______________________________

Victim Recovery Exercises

Complete the following victimization recovery exercises. Use additional paper as needed. Complete each exercise one step at a time. Remember that this can be intense and emotional work. Take your time. Seek support when you need it from the treatment team. Your victim work has only just begun.

Remember:	No matter how badly you may have been abused, it NEVER justifies your choice to abuse someone else.

1. Write a statement to the person(s) who abused you.

2. Write an empathy letter from the abuser to yourself.

3. Write an empathy letter to yourself from yourself.

4. Write down your story. (Or possibly make a recording on audiotape). Talk about your life, as you remember, prior to your victimization. Try to discuss the particulars of your abuse of others. Include information such as:

   - Who abused or abused against you?
   - How old were you?
   - Who could you tell or not tell about the abuse?
   - What happened after the abuse was discovered?
   - How did you hold things inside?
   - How did you learn to shut down your emotions?
   - How did you handle your anger?
   - How does the abuse against you as a child connect to your abusing others today?

   Describe how your victimization affected your feelings and changed your beliefs about yourself and the world. Talk about how your life would have been if you had NOT been abused. It is important to focus on the specific changes that resulted from your victimization.

5. After writing your victimization story, make a list of core negative beliefs that are shown in the story. Then try to create a positive, rational alternative to each negative belief.

Chapter 12
Mental Health and Medications

Beliefs About Mental Illness

Many abusers also have mental health problems and illnesses. Often these mental health problems are treated with psychiatric medication. Many people are afraid to take medication. Some fear that it will change them. Some are worried about side effects. Others are embarrassed to admit that they need a pill to feel right.

This chapter deals with beliefs and issues about mental illness and psychiatric medications. Like everything else, people can have cognitive distortions, false information, and negative beliefs about mental disorders and medication. And the same kinds of cognitive distortion that cause self-defeating and offensive behavior can cause problems for a person who needs psychiatric medication. So a good starting point is to examine your beliefs about mental illness and medications.

Listed below are some common beliefs about mental illness. Please read each statement and rate how much you agree or disagree with each one.

1	2	3	4	5	6	7
Totally Disagree	Disagree Very Much	Disagree Slightly	Neutral	Agree Slightly	Agree Very Much	Totally Agree

____ 1. My mother drank alcohol and/or used drugs.

____ 2. My father drank alcohol and/or used drugs.

____ 3. My immediate relatives have mental problems or emotional problems.

____ 4. I have a mental health diagnosis and I understand it.

____ 5. I think that this diagnosis stuff is a bunch of bull.

1	2	3	4	5	6	7
Totally Disagree	Disagree Very Much	Disagree Slightly	Neutral	Agree Slightly	Agree Very Much	Totally Agree

____ 6. I agree with my diagnosis.

____ 7. I only "play" a role with the doctors so I can get what I want.

____ 8. My emotional problems are just part of growing up.

____ 9. I only act this way in this place. But I'm not really like this.

____ 10. I can tell the difference between self-talk and my cognitive distortions.

____ 11. I hear voices in my head that are not my own self-talk.

____ 12. I know how to get what I want from doctors.

____ 13. I feel depressed most of the time.

____ 14. I never had any problems until I came to this place.

____ 15. A psychiatric diagnosis means that I am crazy.

____ 16. I can get over my mental and emotional problems on my own.

____ 17. If I have a mental illness, I will be in hospitals for the rest of my life.

____ 18. My abuse was caused by my mental problems.

____ 19. People with psychiatric problems commit more abuses.

____ 20. If I take medications, I don't need to work on my negative thinking. The medications will fix it for me.

Beliefs About Psychiatric Medication

Listed below are some common beliefs about psychiatric medications. Please read each statement and rate how much you agree or disagree with each one.

1	2	3	4	5	6	7
Totally Disagree	Disagree Very Much	Disagree Slightly	Neutral	Agree Slightly	Agree Very Much	Totally Agree

____ 1. I only need to take my psychiatric medication when I feel bad.
____ 2. If I need to take psychiatric medications, I must be crazy.
____ 3. Medication is like a crutch.
____ 4. Only weak people take medication.
____ 5. Medication will make me a zombie.
____ 6. I'm not in pain, therefore I do not need medication.
____ 7. Medication has nothing to do with my abusive behavior.
____ 8. There are more bad side effects to medication than good effects.
____ 9. Medication cannot change how I feel.
____ 10. Medications make me feel depressed.
____ 11. When I take medication, it's not me, I am someone else.
____ 12. Medications are too expensive to take after I get out of here, so why take them now.
____ 13. It's embarrassing to take medications all the time.
____ 14. If I take my medications, the medication will control my behavior, not me.
____ 15. Medication will hurt my sex life.
____ 16. I need to control my urges, not the medication.
____ 17. Medications are just like street drugs.
____ 18. I need to solve my problems. Pills won't solve my problems.
____ 19. My family doesn't believe in medications.
____ 20. They just want to control me with medication.
____ 21. If I take medications, I can never drink alcohol, not even socially.
____ 22. Medications make me depressed.
____ 23. If you take medications, you are no longer yourself.
____ 24. I should be able to solve my problems, not use medications to solve my problems.

Understanding My Medication

My psychiatric diagnosis is: ____

____

I can explain my diagnosis in my own words: ________________________________

____

____

____

I am taking the following medication(s) for this diagnosis: ___________________

____

The doctor that explained my medication to me was: _________________________

The other staff that helped to explain my medications to me was/were:_____________

____

The medication is expected to help me in the following ways: __________________

____

____

____

My medication is expected to help my mood and/or behavior in the following way(s):

____

____

____

My psychiatric medication is expected to help me to manage my abusive behavior(s) in the following way(s)____

____

____

____

The possible negative side effects to this medication are: ______________________________

____

____

____

I can explain the possible negative side effects in my own words: ____________________

____

____

____

The major problem with my medication is: ____

____

____

____

Even if it is good for me, the thing that still bothers me about taking medication is: ______

____

____

____

Negative Thoughts About Taking Medication

Write down whatever negative thoughts and beliefs you have about mental illness and psychiatric medications on the left side. Then use what you have learned about changing negative thinking by using rational positive self-talk.

Negative Thoughts and Beliefs	Rational Positive Alternative Beliefs
Example: I'm weak if I have to take pills.	Actually, I'm weak if I don't take my pills because I'm too depressed and tired to do what I like to do.

Medication: Thoughts, Feelings, Behaviors, and Beliefs

Negative Thoughts	Feelings	Behaviors	Beliefs	Rational Alternative Belief
Example: I'm weak because I need to take pills.	Helpless, frustrated.	Act tough and start fights so no one will think I'm weak.	I'm a sick weakling. Everyone hates weaklings.	Taking my medication will help me to be strong by giving me more energy.

Changing Fears of Medication

The doctor and others have tried to explain the value of psychiatric medication for your diagnosis. You have been told about the positive effects of medication on your health and the possible negative side effects. You have considered what it means to you to take medication and considered the reasons that you may not want to take medications. The important question to ask yourself now is:

Do the advantages of taking medication count more than any disadvantages?

You have to be honest with yourself. Medication will not help if you do not fully understand the need for it and agree that it is best for you to take it. Write down any fears or doubts or other reasons that may still bother you about taking medication and rate how strongly you believe it:

Fears, doubts, or reasons that still bother me about medications	Rate belief 1-10
1.	
2.	
3.	
4.	

Now evaluate each reason against taking medication and see which ones are cognitive distortions. Create a rational alternative belief and rate how strongly you believe the new belief. If you have trouble thinking of a rational alternative, ask for help.

Reasons Against	Cognitive Distortions	Positive Rational Alternative	Rate new belief 1-10

Summary

Now that you have completed your Client Workbook, we would like to review some of the topics that you have learned. Remember, if you apply your knowledge from this book, you will lower your risk of engaging in any problem or abusive behavior(s).

Remember to watch and be aware of your negative thinking. Negative thinking and negative words lead you to negative behaviors.

Cognitive Distortions are related to negative thinking. They shade your thinking and distort your view of things. Once you know how your negative thinking and cognitive distortions shade your thoughts you are on your way to not being abusive toward others!

So, you have done that now, and you should feel good about yourself! Remember to control your anger through your cognitive distortion exercises. If you or your family or friends think you are slipping, review these exercises. You have completed them and you should feel good, but remember, "Life happens!"

Remember to review your abuse systems. You have spent time and energy to figure yourself out. Please review this system and congratulate yourself for your efforts!

Aggression begins with your beliefs and your view of the world and yourself. Review your anger system and know that you have completed your system of anger and aggression.

Remember how to change your negative thinking when it happens! Please practice this exercise frequently! Practice your Positive Self Talk- you deserve positive self talk- you completed your workbook!

You have gone from denial to responsibility. You took a negative and made it a therapeutic positive.

The next chapter that you completed was on Healthy Behavior. You learned how to positively experience and express anger and hurt feelings. You mastered how to stop unwanted thoughts and urges. Remember to get out and stay out of your negative belief box! You did it! Right?

If you have had a substance abuse problem, review Chapter 9. You know your relapse prediction score so keep it real! You can do it! You already did!

Chapter 10 on victim empathy was a powerful experience, the interview exercise was real, and so are you! Your work and feelings in this chapter will keep you from becoming abusive or abused! Keep those real feelings alive! It is all you and your work. Feel good about yourself!

If you were a victim of abuse, Chapter 11 helped teach you to overcome your issues and problems. You did this work and it was really hard for you! You were brave enough to deal with your issues…great work!

Finally, Chapter 12 looked at mental health and medication issues. You completed your work and you understand your diagnosis, your issues and your medication. Review this chapter with your clinician and your physician.

You completed your workbook, but your work continues as your life's journey continues. Our best to you!

Our goal in developing and writing this workbook is to help you!

Please send us feedback either way.

Best of life and luck to you!

Jack Apsche

The NEARI Press
New England Adolescent
Research Institute
70 North Summer Street
Holyoke, MA 01040
888.632.7412
603.448.0317
www.nearipress.org

An Introduction to Autism Spectrum Disorders, Sexual Behaviors, & Therapeutic Intervention
by Gary D. Blasingame.
NEARI Press. Paperback, 157 pages.
ISBN 978-1-929657-50-6

Assessing Youth Who Have Sexually Abused: A Primer
by David S. Prescott.
NEARI Press. Paperback, 98 pages.
ISBN 978-1-929657-27-8

Current Applications: Strategies for Working with Sexually Aggressive Youth and Youth with Sexual Behavior Problems
by David S. Prescott
and Robert E. Longo, (Editors).
NEARI Press. Hardcover, 368 pages.
ISBN 978-1-929657-43-8

Current Perspectives: Working with Sexually Aggressive Youth and Youth with Sexual Behavior Problems
by Robert E. Longo
and David S. Prescott (Editors).
NEARI Press. Hardcover, 720 pages.
ISBN 978-1-929657-26-1

Enhancing Empathy
by Robert E. Longo, Laren Bays and Steven Sawyer
NEARI Press. Paperback, 77 pages.
ISBN 978-1-929657-04-9

Evicting the Perpetrator: A Male Survivor's Guide to Recovery from Childhood Sexual Abuse
By Ken Singer.
NEARI Press. Paperback, 268 pages.
ISBN 978-1-929657-46-9

Evolving Residential Work with Children and Families
by James R. Harris, Jr.
NEARI Press. Paperback, 160 pages.
ISBN 978-1-929657-36-0

Growing Beyond: A Workbook for Teenage Girls
by Susan L. Robinson.
NEARI Press. Paperback, 216 pages.
ISBN 978-1-929657-17-9

Growing Beyond Treatment Manual: A Workbook for Sexually Abusive Teenage Girls
by Susan L. Robinson.
NEARI Press. Paperback, 42 pages.
ISBN 978-1-929657-15-5

Lessons from the Lion's Den: Therapeutic Management of Children in Psychiatric Hospitals and Treatment Centers
by Nancy S. Cotton.
NEARI Press. Paperback, 316 pages.
ISBN 978-1-929657-24-7

Men & Anger: Understanding and Managing Your Anger
by Murray Cullen
and Robert E. Longo.
NEARI Press. Paperback, 125 pages.
ISBN 978-1-929657-12-4

Moving Beyond Sexually Abusive Behavior: A Relapse Prevention Curriculum
by Thomas F. Leversee.
NEARI Press. Paperback, 88 pages.
ISBN 978-1-929657-16-2

Moving Beyond: Relapse Prevention Student Manual
by Thomas F. Leversee.
NEARI Press. Paperback, 52 pages.
ISBN 978-1-929657-18-6

New Hope For Youth: Experiential Exercises for Children & Adolescents
by Robert E. Longo
and Deborah P. Longo.
NEARI Press. Paperback, 142 pages.
ISBN 978-1-929657-20-9

Paths To Wellness
by Robert E. Longo.
NEARI Press. Paperback, 144 pages.
ISBN 978-1-929657-13-1

Paths To Wellness en Español!
by Robert E. Longo.
NEARI Press. Paperback, 144 pages.
ISBN 978-1-929657-31-5

The Prevention of Sexual Violence: A Practitioner's Sourcebook
by Keith L. Kaufman (Editor).
NEARI Press. Hardcover, 536 pages.
ISBN 978-1-929657-45-2

Promoting Healthy Childhood Development Today
by James R. Harris, Jr.
NEARI Press. Paperback, 92 pages.
ISBN 978-1-929657-30-8

RESPECT: A Professional Manual
by Tom Keating.
NEARI Press. Paperback, 216 pages.
ISBN 978-1929657-47-1

RESPECT: Student Workbook
by Tom Keating.
NEARI Press. Paperback, 136 pages.
ISBN 978-1-929657-48-3

Responsibility And Self-Management: A Client Workbook of Skills to Learn
by Jack Apsche and Jerry L. Jennings.
NEARI Press. Paperback, 224 pages.
ISBN 978-1-929657-29-2

Responsibility And Self-Management: A Clinician's Manual and Guide for Case Conceptualization
by Jack Apsche and Jerry L. Jennings.
NEARI Press. Paperback, 118 pages.
ISBN 978-1-929657-28-5

Smoothies For The Brain: Brain-Based Strategies To Defuse Behavior Problems in the Classroom
by Penny Cuninggim
and Shannon Chabot.
NEARI Press. Paperback, 48 pages.
ISBN 978-1-929657-35-3

Strong at the Broken Places: Building Resiliency in Survivors of Trauma
by Linda T. Sanford.
NEARI Press. Paperback, 208 pages.
ISBN 978-1-929657-25-4

The Safe Workbook for Youth: New Choices for a Healthy Lifestyle
by John McCarthy and
Kathy MacDonald.
NEARI Press. Paperback, 210 pages.
ISBN 978-1-929657-14-8

Stages of Accomplishment
by Phil Rich. NEARI Press.
Clinician's Manual
Paperback, 96 pages.
ISBN 978-1-929657-41-4
Introduction to Treatment, Stage 1
Paperback, 72 pages.
ISBN 978-1-929657-37-7
Understanding Yourself, Stage 2
Paperback, 96 pages.
ISBN 978-1-929657-38-4
Understanding Dysfunctional Behavior, Stage 3
Paperback, 120 pages.
ISBN 978-1-929657-39-1
Hitting the Target: Making Change Permanent, Stage 4
Paperback, 168 pages.
ISBN 978-1-929657-40-7

The Thursday Group
by PeggyEllen Kleinleder
and Kimber Everson.
NEARI Press. Paperback, 280 pages.
ISBN 978-1-929657-44-5

Try and Make Me! Power Struggles: A Book of Strategies for Adults Who Live and Work with Angry Kids
by Penny Cuninggim.
NEARI Press. Paperback, 112 pages.
ISBN 978-1-929657-23-0

Using Conscience as a Guide: Enhancing Sex Offender Treatment in the Moral Domain
by Niki Delson.
NEARI Press. Paperback, 104 pages.
ISBN 978-1-929657-22-3

Using Conscience as a Guide: Student Manual
by Niki Delson.
NEARI Press. Paperback, 52 pages.
ISBN 978-1-929657-19-3

Who Am I and Why Am I In Treatment?
by Robert E. Longo with Laren Bays
and Steven Sawyer.
NEARI Press. Paperback, 96 pages.
ISBN 978-1-929657-01-8

Why Did I Do It Again & How Can I Stop?
by Robert E. Longo, Laren Bays
and Steven Sawyer
NEARI Press. Paperback, 184 pages.
ISBN 978-1-929657-11-7

For prices and shipping information,
or to order, please call: **888.632.7412**
Find us online at: **www.nearipress.org**